Contents

Author's foreword 2

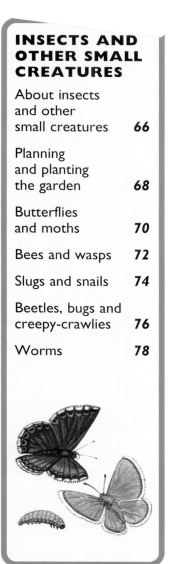

UK Edition

Copyright © 2016 text AG&G Books

The right of A & G Bridgewater to be identified as authors of this work has been asserted by them in accordance with the Copyright, Designs and Patents Act 1988.

Copyright © 2016 illustrations and photographs IMM Lifestyle Books

Copyright © 2016 IMM Lifestyle Books

Designed and created for IMM Lifestyle Books by AG&G Books. Copyright © 2004, 2016 "Specialist" AG&G Books

Design: Glyn Bridgewater; Illustrations: Dawn Brend, Gill Bridgewater, Coral Mula, and Ann Winterbotham; Editor: Alison Copland; Photographs: see page 80

Current Printing (last digit)

10 9 8 7 6 5 4 3

Printed in China

Home Gardener's Wildlife Gardens: Designing, building, planting, developing and maintaining a wildlife garden is published by Creative Homeowner under license with IMM Lifestyle Books.

ISBN: 978-1-58011-730-2

Creative Homeowner®, *www.creativehomeowner.com*, is distributed exclusively in the United Kingdom by Grantham Book Service, Trent Road, Grantham, Lincolnshire, NG31 7XQ.

We are always looking for talented authors. To submit an idea, please send a brief inquiry to acquisitions@foxchapelpublishing.com.

Author's foreword

A look through many of the gardening books published since about the 1930s will show you that gardeners have long been encouraged to poison their so-called 'pests'. The thinking was that if you do not like weeds or wasps, for example, then 'zap' them with chemicals. Fine, you might think – who cares about wasps? Here we come to the heart of it. If we poison, say, wasps, then we are poisoning all of the creatures that feed on them, and in some way skewing the populations of creatures that the wasps feed on. So here we are, after 60 glorious years of chemical warfare, in a situation where the whole interconnected wildlife wheel is faltering and out of kilter.

So what can we do about it? One thing you cannot easily do is look to the internet for advice, because the moment you do a search on almost any garden wildlife creature some chemical company will pop up to sell you their pest-killing products. The good news is that we can start to repair this desperate state of affairs by turning our gardens into wildlife havens. Of course, it will not all be easy, because the moment you stop spraying you will very soon be overrun with bugs. On the other hand, when other creatures get wind of the fact that you have an abundance of just the right bugs, they will come over for a feed, thus re-establishing equilibrium. How do we achieve this? The answer is beautifully simple. Together with your whole family, you can completely give up on chemicals, turn the lawn into a meadow, leave the deadheading of flowers to the birds, abandon the piles of dead leaves to the beetles and bugs, build a hide in the overgrown grass, go wild with planting and pond-building, and just relax and observe nature.

Measurements

Both metric and imperial measurements are given in this book – for example, 1.8 m (6 ft).

SEASONS

Throughout this book, advice is given about seasonal tasks. Because of global and even regional variations in climate and temperature, the four main seasons have been used, with each subdivided into 'early', 'mid-' and 'late' – for example, early spring, mid-spring and late spring. These 12 divisions of the year can be applied to the appropriate calendar months in your local area, if you find this helps.

About the authors

Alan and Gill Bridgewater have gained an international reputation as producers of highly successful gardening and DIY books on a range of subjects, including garden design, ponds and patios, stone and brickwork, decks and decking, and household woodworking. They have also contributed to several international magazines. They live in Rye, East Sussex.

What is a wildlife garden?

A wildlife garden is a place where we – meaning all living organisms – can meet and come together for the common good. Nature is about balance, like a wheel, and if we get the balance right then everything else will follow. At its most basic level, a wildlife garden is a poison-free environment, an eco-sanctuary for plants, birds, mammals, reptiles, insects and many other creatures to live together in harmony the natural way.

Why is wildlife so important?

Water and pondlife

Water is central to the creation of a successful wildlife garden. All manner of creatures live in the water, birds and small mammals come to feed on the creatures in the water, larger animals come to feed on the smaller animals – and so on, round and round. Water is a primary need.

Include as much water as possible – in tubs, water butts, big muddy-edged ponds, and areas of bog garden fringing the pond. These will all attract wildlife.

Birds

Birds are a vital cog in the eco-sanctuary wildlife garden wheel. Certainly, they might nibble away at some of your precious crops, but they look beautiful and will feed on creatures such as aphids and insects.

Don't fret if you see pigeons feeding on your peas, tits feasting on flowers and buds, or rooks eating baby birds. Just focus on the fact that every creature has its natural place.

Mammals, reptiles and fish

You might not like rats, snakes or squirrels, but it is important that your wildlife garden is open to all creatures. Mice will eat snails and slugs, rats will eat mice, snakes will eat rats, large birds will come in and eat snakes – they all have their place in the food chain.

If you are really concerned about snakes or rats, it is best to leave them alone and see how they figure in the overall scheme of things.

Plants

Gardeners normally select specific plants because they look, smell and taste good. For a wildlife garden, you need to introduce plants that will attract creatures as well as being ornamental or beneficial. For example, if you enjoy birds, then you must lure them into your garden by growing plants that both give you pleasure and provide the birds with food in the form of berries, nuts, seeds or flowers.

Butterflies, bees and bugs

It has been said that butterflies, bees and a vast range of 'bugs' are the prime movers of our eco-systems, and that without them our gardens would come to a standstill. You might not like aphids (also known as greenfly and blackfly), but when you see ants systematically 'farming' aphids, and small birds eating aphids, you will begin to see that even the much-hated aphid has its place in the greater scheme of things.

First steps

How can I attract wildlife to my garden?

Once you have established a basic layout – a pond, a variety of shrubs, ground cover, grasses, trees (if space allows), and a selection of nesting boxes – to attract a broad range of wildlife, you need to decide what you specifically want to attract, and shape up the garden accordingly. For example, if you particularly like hedgehogs, find out what they need in the way of shelter and food, and make sure your garden can supply those needs.

Frogs do not need water all year round, but a pond will attract them in the breeding season and they will then probably stay.

There is nothing nicer than a garden full of butterflies on a sunny day. Plants such as buddleia are like magnets for them.

Bees and other insects will pollinate your flowers as well as providing food for birds and other creatures, so encourage them.

Wild meadows, especially if they are low-lying, provide a year-round habitat for a broad range of creatures. Bramble patches also make safe, impenetrable homes for birds, mice, rabbits and larger mammals such as badgers and foxes.

Water gardens are an absolute haven for many types of wildlife, from sparkling damselflies to graceful birds and amphibians.

POSITIVE PLANNING

Positive neglect

An easy option is just to let a part of your garden run wild and go back to nature. Such an area will soon become overrun with the 'unwanted' plants that are common to your area – such as nettles, docks and wild grasses – but they will also become a haven for wildlife. These wild corners also become 'jungles' for your children to play in – great places to build camps and hideaways, and to see nature close up.

Entrance to wild garden

Creating wildlife food chains

Nuts

Berries

Seeds

The wonderful thing about a wildlife garden is the fact that everything you plant will start off a food chain. Squirrels, mice and birds will feed on nuts and seeds; harvest mice particularly like berries; rabbits eat grasses and nuts. Therefore, once you have planted species that produce nuts, berries and seeds, and once the year-round growing, flowering and fruiting cycle associated with these plants is established, these areas will become home to insects, worms, slugs and snails, and these will in turn attract the larger creatures, including badgers, foxes and moles. You might not particularly want gnats, slugs and bugs, but these difficult-to-like creatures will in turn attract snakes, badgers and birds – all the creatures that most of us want in our wildlife gardens.

Wild water gardens

A small 'natural' pond – it need be no more than a little hole in the ground filled with water – will soon become a haven for all manner of insects, aquatic plants, frogs, toads and newts. This type of pond will soon become a back-to-nature playground for the whole family to enjoy. You can either introduce plants and fish or sit back and let native wildlife take over. If you introduce fish, however, they will eat other pondlife (see page 26).

A small, natural pond quickly attracts wildlife

Log piles

In times past, when there were large areas of forest and woodland, there were huge supplies of tree stumps and decaying wood that gave a home to wildlife. Some beetles lay their eggs in rotten wood, there are grubs that eat wood, there are wasps that nest in decaying wood, slugs and snails that live under old logs, and vast numbers of worms, ants, centipedes, beetles and bugs that need to live in, on, under or near decaying wood. To recreate this habitat, pile up some logs and let them slowly decay.

HEDGES

A garden hedge is a great option for wildlife. A good, solid, traditional mixed hedge of hawthorn, box and dog rose makes the perfect sheltered place for wildlife to thrive. Birds will nest and eat the berries and bugs, hedgehogs and mice will live and feed in its shelter, snakes, lizards, frogs and toads will be encouraged by its cover and by the food source, butterflies will shelter and feed in its cover, and so on.

Hawthorn, Dog Rose and Box

HEDGING GUIDE

- *Buxus sempervirens* (**Box**) – Plant 1.5 m (5 ft) apart in autumn.

- *Crataegus monogyna* (**Hawthorn**) – Plant 45 cm (18 in) apart in autumn.

- *Hedera* spp. (**Ivy**) – Just let it grow in with the hedge; it is good for butterflies, birds, mice and ants.

- *Ilex* spp. (**Holly**) – Plant 60 cm (2 ft) apart in late summer or early autumn to provide nesting sites.

- *Ligustrum* spp. (**Privet**) – Plant 30 cm (1 ft) apart at any time of year to provide good cover for small birds.

- *Rosa canina* (**Dog Rose**) – Grow as part of a mixed hedge.

A town garden

Is my town garden too small?

Asmall town garden might not be a good haven for large animals, but it will attract everything from mice, moles, frogs and toads through to dozens of different types of birds and thousands of minute insects and grubs. It is often said that 'small is beautiful', and many of the tiny creatures that you will find in your garden lead fascinating and mysterious lives that, as yet, we know very little about. Who knows what might be lurking at the bottom of your garden?

Even the smallest water feature will provide a home for wild creatures.

KEY FEATURES OF A TOWN WILDLIFE GARDEN

↗ *A small balcony garden packed with flowering plants will provide a haven for all manner of birds and insects.*

↗ *You can maximize your garden's wildlife potential by filling every nook and corner with plants and structures.*

↗ *The more berry- and seed-bearing plants you include, the more creatures will come into the garden for food. Try to leave small piles of debris to give home to insects.*

WATER FEATURES

Dry, barren gardens work for some creatures in some areas of the world, but if you really want to increase your wildlife options (the diversity of the creatures) then you need water – a sump or a half-barrel filled with water, for example, or a pond. While a little natural-looking wild pond hidden away in a well-planted corner is likely to be the best option, even the smallest of water features will do. If you have doubts about this, just fill a bucket with water and leave it in the garden for a couple of weeks. By then it will be alive with minute insects and larvae, and if you keep looking long enough you will spot all manner of larger creatures coming in for a drink and a feast.

PLANTS FOR FOOD

Wildlife gardens are, from the animals' and insects' point of view, primarily about shelter and food. The more shelter and food you provide, the more creatures will come in. Start by planting species that will provide birds with food in the winter. The cycle goes something like this: you plant a good range of berry- and seed-bearing plants (ones that are common in your area), the birds come in to feed, leaves and pips fall, mice and other small mammals feed on the debris, smaller insects and worms feed on the waste, and so on.

DESIGNS

Design for a town orchard meadow garden

➔ You might only have a long narrow garden with a few trees, a formal pond at one end, and a neatly tailored central lawn, but it does not have to be like that. This long, narrow town garden draws inspiration from the traditional orchard meadow. The important ingredients here are the fruit trees, the long grass with meadow flowers to the side, a bark-covered area for sitting, large logs, and a small natural-looking pond surrounded by irises. Mow paths through the grass and plant the pond with native or other species.

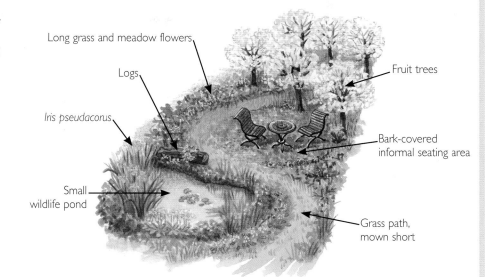

Long grass and meadow flowers

Logs

Fruit trees

Iris pseudacorus

Bark-covered informal seating area

Small wildlife pond

Grass path, mown short

Design for a traditional cottage garden

➔ Build the basic features into the design – the well or pond, the lawn, the vegetable area and so on – and then cram in as many plants as possible. The vegetable beds may look a bit scruffy and there may be weeds at the back of the borders, but just think how the plant debris is going to bring in insects, worms, bugs, beetles and birds.

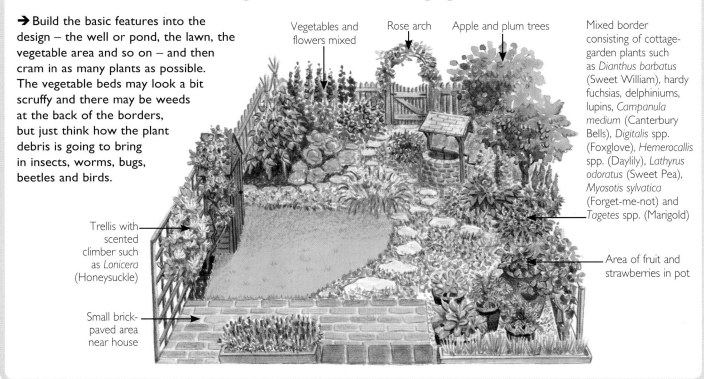

Vegetables and flowers mixed

Rose arch

Apple and plum trees

Mixed border consisting of cottage-garden plants such as *Dianthus barbatus* (Sweet William), hardy fuchsias, delphiniums, lupins, *Campanula medium* (Canterbury Bells), *Digitalis* spp. (Foxglove), *Hemerocallis* spp. (Daylily), *Lathyrus odoratus* (Sweet Pea), *Myosotis sylvatica* (Forget-me-not) and *Tagetes* spp. (Marigold)

Trellis with scented climber such as *Lonicera* (Honeysuckle)

Small brick-paved area near house

Area of fruit and strawberries in pot

HINTS AND TIPS

- You could reduce the mown lawn to a minimum, so as to maximize the size of the more fruitful borders.
- Leave a space behind the trees that is big enough for a good-sized compost heap.
- Remember that wild creatures need good cover so that they can move freely from one area to another.
- Even the smallest of ponds will support wildlife; for example, we have a sump pond about 1 m (3½ ft) square that is full of newts.

- Leave a layer of debris – cabbage leaves, fallen fruit, hedge clippings – in one corner of the garden to encourage small creatures to take up residence.
- Put up a feeding table, and one or two nesting boxes.
- Allow fallen fruit to rot down where it falls.
- Leave small untidy areas so that creatures can safely exist without being disturbed.
- Even the smallest water feature will give a home to a variety of wild creatures.

A country garden

What can I expect to see?

As you might guess, a garden located in the countryside will attract a greater range of wildlife than one in the middle of a town. The type of creatures you are likely to see, however, will depend upon the precise location of your rural retreat. In addition to the locally common species of birds, insects and mammals, you might be lucky enough to encounter more 'exotic' animals such as snakes, foxes, deer and wildcats.

HEDGES

A good solid mixed hedge is essential, planted with as many different species as possible (see page 5). A hedge of this character will provide a whole range of creatures with shelter and food. Ideally, the hedge needs to ring and/or intersect your property and link to your neighbours, so that creatures have a corridor, a sort of unbroken belt that allows them to move safely from one area to another – from meadows to woodland, woodland to wetlands, and so on.

WATER

Water is a vital element in a wildlife garden, and can be in the form of anything from small sumps, fancy ponds and large natural ponds to vast lakes and trickling streams. Wildlife does not care about the shape and depth, as long as the water is free from chemicals. It also does not matter too much if the pond or stream becomes a bit stagnant and/or completely silts and evolves into a bog garden, because there are always going to be creatures that prefer it that way.

If you are serious about wanting wildlife, a small stream or pond is a must.

KEY FEATURES OF A COUNTRY WILDLIFE GARDEN

↗ *Plants that bear good numbers of seeds and berries are vital – choose varieties that will provide food throughout the four seasons.*

↗ *A small, natural-looking pond will be a joy to the eye and attract a variety of creatures.*

↗ *A small orchard-type scenario, complete with moist areas, long grass and fallen fruit, will provide food.*

↗ *For some creatures, such as beetles, a decaying log will be a place to breed, live, feed and die.*

↗ *Evergreen shrubs provide food and shelter in the winter and cool, moist cover in the summer.*

DESIGN FOR A WILDLIFE GARDEN

⭷If you look at the town orchard meadow illustration (page 7 top), you will see that the country design builds on the basic theme by adding hedges, larger areas of meadow grass, more trees, a bigger pile of logs, a bigger pond and a bog garden. If your particular location has rocky outcrops or a stream running through it, for example, you may need to modify the basic design to suit.

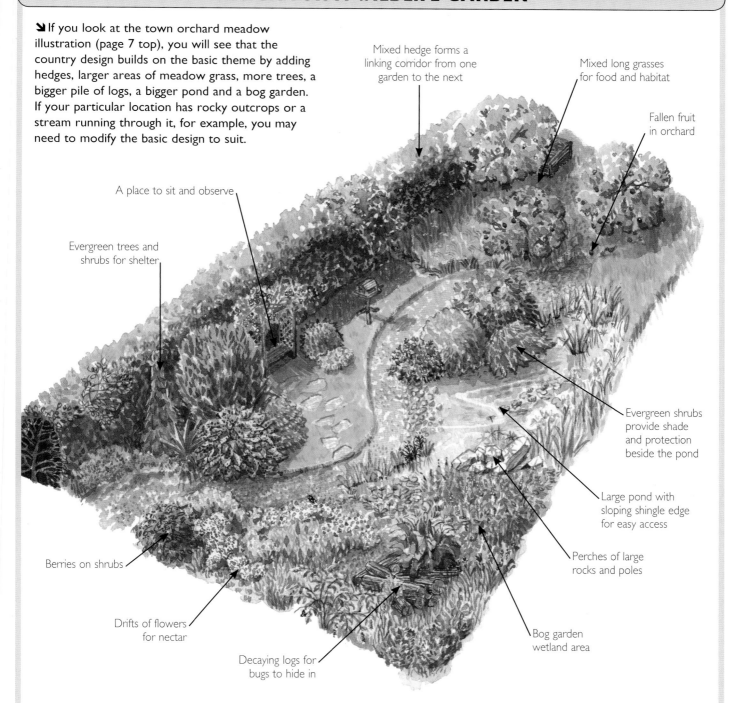

Mixed hedge forms a linking corridor from one garden to the next

Mixed long grasses for food and habitat

Fallen fruit in orchard

A place to sit and observe

Evergreen trees and shrubs for shelter

Evergreen shrubs provide shade and protection beside the pond

Large pond with sloping shingle edge for easy access

Berries on shrubs

Perches of large rocks and poles

Drifts of flowers for nectar

Bog garden wetland area

Decaying logs for bugs to hide in

Hints and tips

• You could enlarge the pond and concentrate on pondlife and large mammals.
• You could enlarge the orchard and include a bog garden.
• Woodchips are good for paths and patios, and when broken down they can be put on the vegetable garden as a mulch.
• Remember that if children will use the garden you must make sure the pond is safe. If you have concerns about ponds and small children, one option is to build a large pond, turn it into a bog garden, and then turn it back into a pond when the children are older and able to look after themselves.
• You could build a shelter – perhaps a treehouse – and camouflage it, so as to make a hide from which to watch your wildlife without it seeing you and taking fright (see pages 15 and 39).

Wildflowers and other plants

Does wildlife prefer native plants?

The idea of plants being 'native' or 'indigenous' to your local area or country is, to a great extent, a fallacy, since most of the world's plant species have evolved from common ancestors. As for wildlife preferring these so-called native plants, generally speaking creatures do not care how long your plants have been in the country, as long as there is a wide variety and plenty of them. For plants that will thrive in your area, see what does well in your neighbours' gardens.

CHOOSING PLANTS

When selecting 'wildlife-friendly' plants, do not start by loading yourself down with lists of unwieldy botanical names, but do a bit of research into what your preferred wildlife visitors need in the way of shelter, protection and food. Once you know that this type of bird likes these seeds and those berries, and that snake likes a certain sort of cover, and such a beetle likes one sort of flowerhead rather than another, then you will have a good idea of which trees, grasses, bushes and flowers to choose. When you have thriving plants that provide year-round shelter and food for your favourite birds, beetles and snakes, then plenty of bird-, beetle- and snake-loving animals will also be sure to follow.

TIPS ON PLANTING

- Try to choose a good range of plants so that you have a long flowering season, different shapes and colours of flowers, different bark textures and so on.
- Plant in large drifts so that animals are able to move from one area to another without being exposed to predators.
- Try to keep your area of mown lawn to a minimum.
- Plant lots of different grasses.
- Plant swathes of your favourite plants, irrespective of whether you think of them as wildlife-friendly.
- Choose plants that are long established in your area.

Aim for as many different plants as possible so that the ground is completely covered, providing privacy and shelter for creatures.

PLANTING SCHEMES

This small front-yard garden has been planted for maximum impact, with plenty of cover and lots of seeds and berries.

Group plant pots and containers so that there are little secret areas between them for insects and small mammals to feed and forage in.

Lonicera japonica

Berberis thunbergii
'Atropurpurea Nana'

Phormium   Camellia

Rhododendron

Rudbeckia

Skimmia
japonica

Erica carnea   Pinus mugo (Pumilio Group)   Hosta   Lavandula

Alchemilla mollis

Vinca minor

This border scheme has been cleverly designed so that there are plants at all levels and the ground is entirely covered.

PLANTS FOR PARTICULAR CREATURES

This list will give you some idea of what the wild creatures in the garden will prefer in the way of plants.

- **Birds** like plants that produce plenty of berries and seeds, such as cotoneaster, hawthorn, blackberry, cherry and sunflower (see page 37).
- **Small mammals** like berries, seeds, grasses, acorns and nuts, but they also like the birds, eggs, grubs, bugs and insects that are attracted to the berries and seeds (see also page 55).
- **Reptiles** eat berries and seeds, but for the most part they are after the small mammals and bugs that come in for the berries and seeds. With this in mind, you could plant lots of ground cover to keep both the mammals and reptiles happy (see also page 55).
- **Butterflies, moths, bees and other insects** are attracted by buddleia, stinging nettles, lilac, lavender, foxgloves and other 'cottage-garden' plants, as well as some night-scented plants such as honeysuckle, evening primrose and verbena (see page 69).

CAUTION

Be warned that if you are going to encourage your 'pretty' wildlife top-ten favourites – birds, rabbits, mice and so on – then you are, by the very nature of things, also inviting in larger animals that will have their own top-ten tasty list.

Do your best to keep 'barren' areas, such as lawns and paths, to a minimum. Replace them as far as possible with dense planting.

Cats and dogs

*Will my pets
scare away
the wildlife?*

Current research suggests that in the UK and the USA domestic cats make many millions of wildlife catches a year, of which about 20–30 per cent are birds. The research goes on to say that a lot of these birds would probably have died anyway. The truth is, however, that cats – and to a lesser extent dogs – do have a negative impact on garden wildlife, but this is a complex problem with no simple answer. The best you can do is care and protect your own patch.

When hunting small mammals or birds, a cat is merely following its natural instincts, so try to deter it rather than blame it.

Views on cats in the garden range from the 'leave-poor-pussy-alone' lobby through to the 'ban-the-killer-cat' extremists. All we can say for sure is that a cat will kill any creature it can catch – including birds, snakes, lizards and fish. We cannot blame the cat, because it is only acting naturally, and humans have elected to keep cats as domestic pets. The best thing to do is try to figure out how to outwit the cat. If you spend time making sure that your garden is heavily planted with wildlife-friendly vegetation, with as many shrubs, trees and ground-cover plants as you can stuff into the plot, and if you positively encourage a full range of wildlife, then the cat will simply slot into its place in the scheme of things.

CAT DETERRENTS

You could put up an electric fence, and install all manner of expensive machines that variously buzz, ping, hum and squirt, and you could surround your house with a cat-proof maze of ground chilli peppers, bottles filled with water, lumps of lion dung, and so on, but why would you want to, when a good number of these so-called cat deterrents would, if they worked, deter the very wildlife that you are trying to attract? If you feel that you absolutely must get a deterrent, then get yourself a small, noisy dog, one that will scare off cats without being a danger to wildlife. As for having a cat of your own, research suggests that a wildlife garden and cats are a bad mix.

DOGS IN A WILDLIFE GARDEN

While cats tend to be blamed for the decline in bird populations, dogs are generally thought of as being nature's friend. Perhaps this has to do with imagery that links dogs with various traditional country pursuits. The fact is that if you have a large, boisterous dog bounding about the garden it will at least deter nest-building birds and scare off all the shy little animals that like a quiet life.

As for comparing dogs and cats, the truth is that dogs do not generally climb over fences and creep about in other people's gardens, and they can at the very least be trained to stay within the confines of their own patch.

This pretty pussycat likes nothing better than eating birds, mice, rats and rabbits.

Dogs will scare off some wild creatures, but are very unlikely to kill them.

PREVENTION IS BETTER THAN CURE

If you put food scraps out for birds, at least make sure that they are put on a table that is well clear of the ground, in a situation where cats cannot easily creep up unnoticed. Stop putting shop-bought bird food out in the same spot each time – because it makes the cat's life easier by luring in birds and other wildlife. Plant plenty of prickly-leaved plants around the garden.

If you have a problem with a dog scaring wildlife, the chances are that it is your own dog doing the scaring. If you want to have a wildlife garden and a dog, you will need to keep the dog away from the wildlife area by building an outside run. The sight and sound of the dog in a run will not actively encourage wildlife to your patch, but it will at least ensure that the said dog is not tearing through the undergrowth and generally frightening away all the creatures in its path. You could also train your dog so that it quietly does your bidding.

POINTS TO CONSIDER

- There is evidence to show that various garden bird species are on the decline, but there is no firm evidence that pins the blame on cats.

- Remember, when you are looking at the various electronic scare devices available, that the back-up literature about the number of birds killed and the dangers of cats in the garden is likely to be biased.

- Current research suggests that birds and animals flee when dogs approach and that visiting wild animals will always be alarmed by dogs, simply because they never get the chance to become accustomed to their presence. If this is correct, you must face up to the fact that your dog will, more than likely, scare away exotic wildlife visitors.

- On the plus side, while a dog might well scare away some part of the wildlife in your garden, it will probably not kill it.

- We all have to make choices, so you might have to decide that you are happy to have a dog and limited wildlife.

Children

*What about
my kids?*

Most children adore wildlife. They are fascinated by creepy-crawlies, they love exploring secret wet and muddy places, they enjoy being hidden away and watching wild creatures acting naturally, and they are enthralled by all the dramatic life-and-death happenings. As far as your young family is concerned, your wildlife garden will be a wonderful, life-shaping experience that should not be missed. Involve them from the start in your wildlife garden project.

The bright red colour and black spots of ladybirds will captivate most children.

How to record sightings or finds

Take photographs from a hide – You could build a hide (see opposite), show your kids how to use a digital camera, and leave them be. Once they appreciate that a good part of taking wildlife shots is about being secret, there will be no stopping them.

Make plaster casts – This is a good way of saving footprints such as badger tracks (see method opposite).

Make drawings and pressings – If your funds do not run to a camera, or you prefer a more direct, hands-on approach, making drawings and pressing leaves and flowers is a good option. Keep it simple, using just a fat pad of plain paper, brown paper, lick-and-stick tape, and soft pencils.

Create a showcase – Your kids will need a little display case in which to keep and display their finds. A salvaged item such as a glass-fronted cupboard with two or three shelves would be ideal. Make little labels that record the name of the item, and the date and place it was found.

Join a group – If your children become interested in a particular sighting or find, such as a rare bird or an unusual bug, a good idea is to join a local group. Contact your local wildlife organization for details of specialist groups in your area.

LEARNING THROUGH NATURE

In a wildlife garden, your children will be able to see animals fighting, eating, mating, being born and dying. Once they know how food is grown, how eggs hatch, and why all the animals do what they do, then all their natural feelings of wonderment, enjoyment and involvement will follow. Kids love collecting natural objects such as snake skins, bird pellets, bones and feathers. A good way of involving them in the wildlife garden is to tap into their collecting and exploring interests, and show them how to record their finds (see above).

You must always supervise your children when they are exploring the watery areas of the garden, which can be dangerous.

Warning – always be aware of the dangers

Children are fascinated by water, but even the smallest pond can be a killer. If you have toddlers, or small kids that cannot swim, then if you have a pond in the garden you must watch over them at all times. While you might be fairly certain that your own children have an understanding and respect for water, you have no way of knowing how visiting kids are going to react if they slip or fall into the water, so constant vigilance is absolutely essential.

Other risks lurk in the form of animals and plants. An injured badger or a handful of poisonous berries can pose a real danger. Again, you may not have to worry so much about your own kids, because by the time you let them loose on their own they will have a good idea of all the dangers, but visiting children must be supervised at all times.

HOW TO MAKE PLASTER CASTS OF ANIMAL TRACKS

Having found a track, carefully remove any loose sticks and leaves from around it. Use a 5 cm (2 in) wide strip of cardboard to build a circular 'wall' around the track. Fix the overlapping ends of the cardboard with a paper clip and press the ring into the soil, taking care not to damage the track as you do so. Mix up some plaster of Paris (two cups of plaster to one cup of water) and stir until you have a thick, but still slightly runny, mix. Carefully pour the mix into the cardboard mould so that it fills and gradually tops up the track marks. Lift the plaster when it is hard, leave it for a couple of days, and then use a soft brush and running water to clean away the debris.

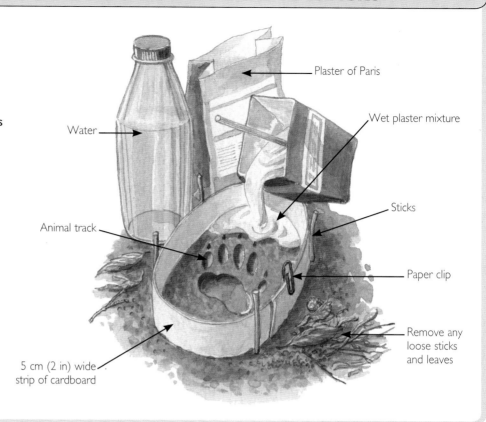

Plaster of Paris

Wet plaster mixture

Water

Sticks

Animal track

Paper clip

Remove any loose sticks and leaves

5 cm (2 in) wide strip of cardboard

HOW TO MAKE A HIDE

A hide is a little shelter that is disguised to look like its surroundings.

- Cut or find eight wooden poles – four that are about 1.8 m (6 ft) long, and four that are about 1.2 m (4 ft) long.
- Set the four longer poles in the ground so as to make a 90 x 90 cm (3 x 3 ft) square.
- Use string to lash the four shorter poles horizontally to the tops of the longer poles, so that you have a stable structure.
- Cover the structure with plastic sheet topped with old sacking or canvas – or anything that looks dirty and camouflaged.
- Cover the whole structure with leaves, branches or grass so that it blends in with your garden, and cut a spyhole at a height to suit.

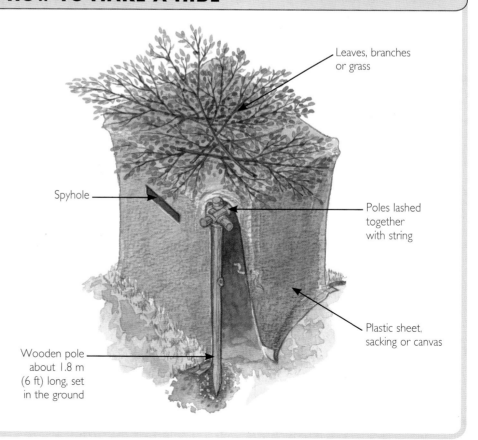

Leaves, branches or grass

Spyhole

Poles lashed together with string

Plastic sheet, sacking or canvas

Wooden pole about 1.8 m (6 ft) long, set in the ground

About water gardens

Why is a water garden desirable?

Even the smallest garden can host a wildlife pond. If you leave a tub, bucket, half-barrel or butt of water in the garden for a month, it will turn green with algae and you will find a variety of aquatic larvae in the water. After about six months, creatures such as birds, frogs, mice and lizards will come to it to feed. Whether a pond is small, medium or huge, it is a diverse ecosystem, and every wildlife garden will benefit from having one.

TYPES OF PONDS

Having said that all ponds are good, some are undoubtedly better than others. Well-planted, muddy-bottomed, natural-looking ponds – where the garden runs down through uneven-edged shallows and on into the water – are better for wildlife than unplanted, minimalist, tiled, formal fishponds. Deep, medium-clear water is always better than a murky, shallow sludge. Ponds sited in partial sun do better than ones in either full sun or full shade. Ponds overstocked with fish are not as good, and a large pond will inevitably host a larger range of wildlife than a small one.

MAINTAINING AN ECOSYSTEM

- An ecosystem is the interaction between living things and their environment. For a successful wildlife pond, a balance must be found between your preferences – say, for clear water, lots of fish and tidiness – and the requirements of the ecosystem to keep itself in balance.

- If you introduce too many fish, they will eat too many small creatures – say, all the water fleas – and the algae will grow out of control.
- Do not be in too much of a hurry to add mains water from the tap, because it contains a variety of minerals and salts that encourage the growth of algae.
- Be tolerant. If you want to have birds visiting your garden, then you must have gnats, hoverflies and all the other buzzing and flitting creatures on which they feed.

HOW A WILDLIFE POND ECOSYSTEM WORKS

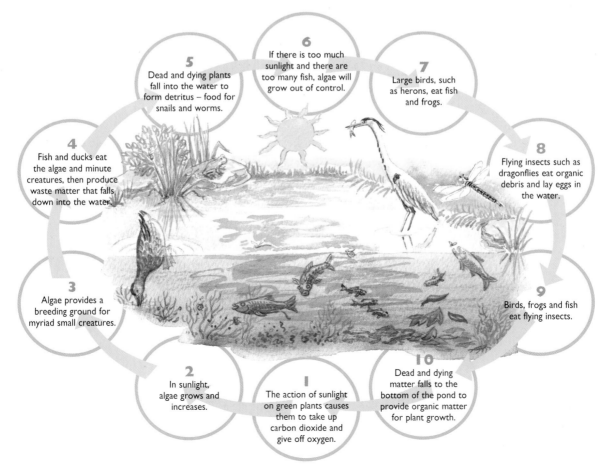

5 Dead and dying plants fall into the water to form detritus – food for snails and worms.

6 If there is too much sunlight and there are too many fish, algae will grow out of control.

7 Large birds, such as herons, eat fish and frogs.

4 Fish and ducks eat the algae and minute creatures, then produce waste matter that falls down into the water.

8 Flying insects such as dragonflies eat organic debris and lay eggs in the water.

3 Algae provides a breeding ground for myriad small creatures.

9 Birds, frogs and fish eat flying insects.

2 In sunlight, algae grows and increases.

1 The action of sunlight on green plants causes them to take up carbon dioxide and give off oxygen.

10 Dead and dying matter falls to the bottom of the pond to provide organic matter for plant growth.

WATER CREATURES AND PLANTS

When the water garden is established, eventually large birds such as herons will come in to feed on the fish and frogs.

The design of this pond, with plenty of lush vegetation around the edges, allows creatures to move from the land to the water without being overly exposed.

Frogs feed on a broad range of insects. They may also use the pond for breeding, giving you both spawn and tadpoles to observe.

If you have a fairly large area of water, ducks may come in to feed on algae, selected plants and minute creatures.

Emergent plants allow flying creatures such as dragonflies to settle near the water.

Water-garden design

If there is water at the heart of your garden – anything from a sump pond or large natural pond to a stream or bog garden – you will be giving a home to creatures that, but for the water, would not be able to live there. The type of water garden you create will depend on your particular situation. Here we show a range of ideas for pond design, together with planting suggestions. Just keep in mind that lots of water equates with lots of wildlife.

A DESIGN FOR A WILDLIFE POND

Trees with nesting boxes

Sunflower seeds

Hedge

Bird table

Fruit trees

Rustic pergola

Insect-attracting plants

Long grass

Logs for bugs

Large stones for frogs and birds

Water plants

Bog garden

Natural appearance
To attract a broad range of creatures, a good pond needs to be as natural as possible, with shallow, muddy margins, a good range of trees, bushes and ground-cover plants, piles of decaying wood and leaves – all the messy components that you would expect to find around a natural pond.

Is it right for you?
By its very nature, a successful wildlife pond area will be shady and muddy underfoot, will look slightly uncared for, and will generally be alive with gnats and wildlife. Is this going to suit you and your family?

Variations to consider
If you particularly like meadow ponds, fewer trees, taller grasses, shingle rather than bark, or any other variation, then go for it. You could then miss out on, say, woodland creatures, but you will still attract wildlife.

DESIGN GUIDELINES

- Although ideally you need a good-sized site – the bigger the better – it could be managed on a small plot of, say, 25 m (80 ft) square.

- The area of water needs to be as large as possible.

- Create a bog garden to the side of the pond.

- You need trees around the site – the more the better.

- Spread and heap woodchips, crushed bark or leaf litter over the ground to make paths.

- Put piles of logs at various places throughout the site.

- Plant the pond with a good range of water plants (see pages 24–25).

BOG GARDENS

A bog garden can be created in the soggy, low-lying areas around the edges of a pond or lake (see pages 22–23). The soil needs to be wet, with the underlying water free-moving rather than stagnant. If you like water-loving wildlife such as frogs, toads, newts and snakes, you will enjoy a bog garden. There are bog plants suitable for every situation: high bog areas that partly dry out in high summer; middle bog areas that are always slightly moist; and low bog areas that are more water than bog. Some plants are so adaptable that they thrive in places that are liable to extremes of both flood and drought.

MORE WATER-GARDEN DESIGNS

Water garden for a small plot

↘ There are three basic elements to this design: a wild pond, a bog garden fed by rainwater run-off from the pond, and dense planting on the exposed side away from the house.

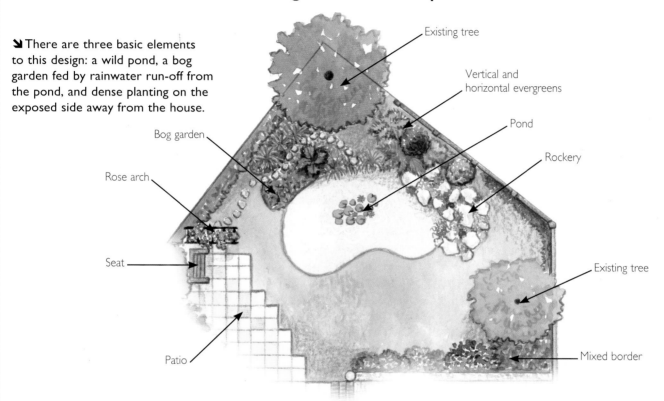

Existing tree

Vertical and horizontal evergreens

Pond

Rockery

Bog garden

Rose arch

Seat

Patio

Existing tree

Mixed border

Beachside edging

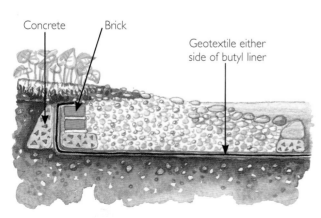

Concrete   Brick

Geotextile either side of butyl liner

↗ This pond has been built with a flexible liner and a concrete and brick ring foundation. Note how the liner is hidden from view. Use pebbles to create the beach area.

Bog-garden edging

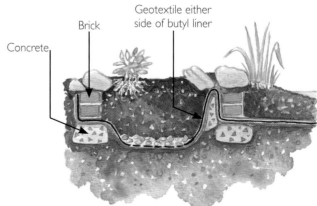

Geotextile either side of butyl liner

Brick

Concrete

↗ Here the pond is edged with a mixture of bog area and stone. The overflow from the pond is contained by a butyl-lined trench, and the liner has been pierced for drainage.

Building a wildlife pond

How can I make it look natural?

The trick with creating a natural-looking pond is to build the edging so that all traces of the construction materials are completely hidden from view. For example, with a bit of forward planning, it is easily possible to conceal the edges of a butyl pond liner. Here, while you cannot see anything on the surface other than plants, rocks and earth, below the surface there is a concrete and brick foundation that holds everything in place.

DESIGN COMPONENTS

For maximum impact and to attract a broad range of creatures, a good wildlife pond needs to be as large as possible, with lots of ground cover, trees and all the decaying debris that such a scenario produces. A design that draws inspiration from a woodland glade is a good option. The components are a small, level area of grass or woodchips, a pond, a meandering path, a place to sit, trees all around, and lots of decaying wood and leaves.

CARE AND MAINTENANCE

- The pond will need to be cleaned out at the start and finish of the season. Remove debris and pile it up at the water's edge so that it can rot down, and so that water creatures can make it back to the water.
- Clean the bird boxes out in winter.
- Make sure the paths are clear, so that you can enjoy the garden and see all the various bird boxes.

An area of low-angled shingle beach allows easy access to the water, and is a safer option if children and elderly people use the garden.

Children and elderly people

A garden like this is going to be shady with lots of wood and leaf debris underfoot, and of course the water. You will attract wildlife, but there will be insects, a fair amount of mud at the edges of the pond, and an apparently uncared-for look. If you have a family, say with small children and elderly people, then is a garden of this character going to be safe? It is true that you will have to spend extra time watching your children and generally making sure that they are out of harm's way, and elderly people will have to take extra care, but just think how exciting it will be for your kids and elderly relatives to watch wildlife in reality rather than on the television.

A small island, together with a shelter, gives ducks and other water birds a safe retreat where land predators cannot reach them.

HOW TO BUILD A WILDLIFE POND

↘ The easiest option is to build the pond using a flexible butyl liner protected with layers of geotextile. Although the building procedures are easy enough, it is the details that help to give the total area its character – the shape and depth of the pond, the size of the bog area, the number and depth of the planting shelves, the height of the pond-edge wall, the number of trees, and so on. If you get the details right, then success will be sure to follow.

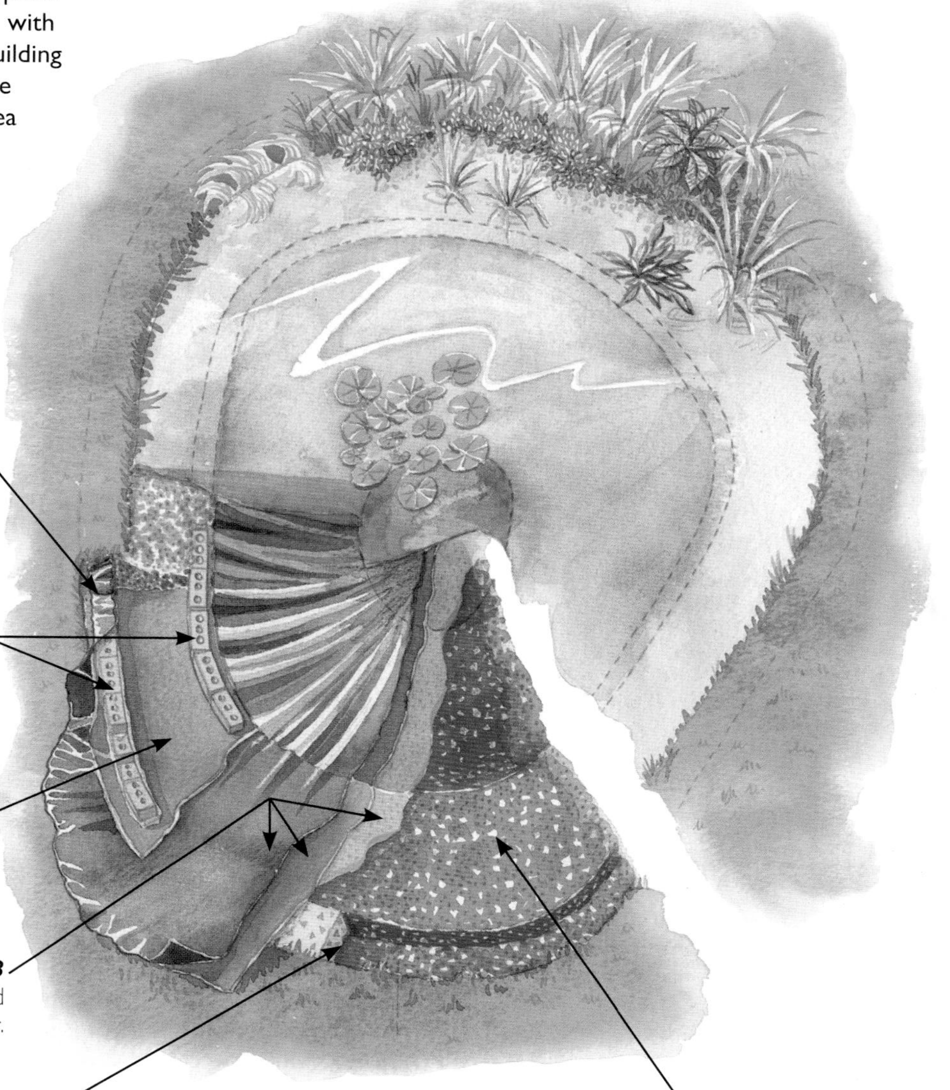

Step 6
Trim back the geotextile and fold the butyl liner up and over the top of the wall. Cover both the wall and the planting shelf with earth.

Step 5
Build a three-brick-high wall on the concrete ring foundation at the edge of the pond. Lay a row of dry bricks along the edge of the planting shelf.

Step 4
Cover the edge of the butyl liner with another layer of geotextile, so that it runs down to the edge of the planting shelf.

Step 3
Cover the site with a layer of sand, followed by the geotextile and the butyl liner.

Step 2
Dig a trench, 20 cm (8 in) wide and 20 cm (8 in) deep, to establish the edge of the pond, and fill it with a 15 cm (6 in) layer of concrete.

➔ This illustrates the pond construction method described above and shows how the liner is cleverly concealed from view.

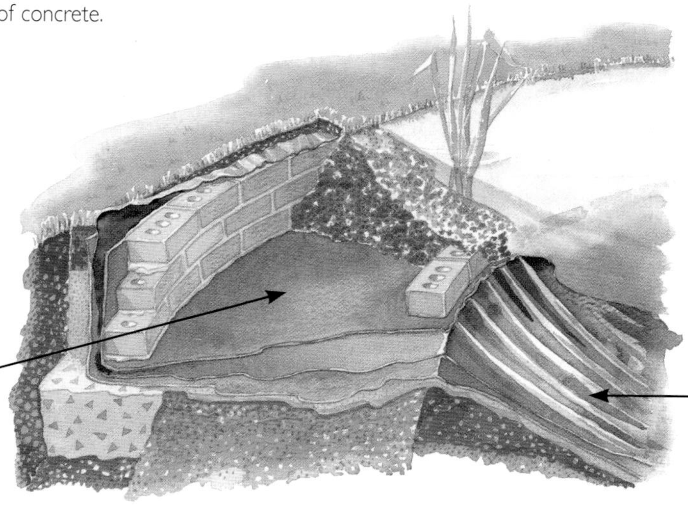

Planting shelf

Cross-section detail

Step 1
Having created a design that suits your garden, mark out the basic shape on the ground using string and pegs, a spray marker, or even sand poured from a bottle. Dig out the hole to a depth of 75 cm (2½ ft) in the centre, and sculpt the earth around the edges to make the planting shelf and a 3-in-1 slope down from the edge of the shelf.

3-in-1 slope

Building a bog garden

Natural ponds generally have areas of soggy, low-lying bog around the water's edge, which are packed with rushes, irises, the nests of water birds, frogs, newts and so on. Characteristically, these areas very rarely dry out, they are wet and difficult underfoot, and conditions are such that the underlying water is free-flowing rather than stagnant. In a wildlife garden, a bog garden is an artificial replication of a stretch of pondside plant life.

Lythrum salicaria (Purple Loosestrife) is a wonderful option for a bog garden – it thrives in well-watered, muddy areas.

Boggy areas may be difficult for humans underfoot, but they are perfect for certain types of plant and for associated wildlife.

DESIGN COMPONENTS

A bog garden can be built around the edge of a wildlife pond so that it benefits from pond overflow and seepage; or, if the garden is too small for a pond, it can be built as a feature in its own right. The primary components are boggy soil (always wet but never stagnant), lots of shade and dense, lush planting. If you are trying to keep costs to a minimum, you could line the bog garden with lots of recycled plastic bags, well overlapped.

VARIATIONS TO CONSIDER

If you enjoy the notion of a pond and bog garden, but have decided for safety's sake to keep water to a minimum, you could build two small ponds, one at a slightly higher level than the other, with a large area of bog garden in between. Water is directed into the higher or 'feeder' pond from the rest of the garden, then overflows down and through the bog garden, and finally drains into the lower or 'sump' pond. With this scenario, you can have most of the wildlife advantages of a pond and bog garden without actually having a large area of water.

Children and elderly people

The average bog garden is not as dangerous as a pond – you cannot drown in it – but the ground is nevertheless soft and squidgy. Bog gardens are usually set close to ponds and at a lower level than most of the garden, so they are by nature slippery and treacherous underfoot. If you are worried about children or elderly folk, you can build dry high-ground woodchip walks that cross the bog garden, and/or put up a fence around the bog garden.

HOW TO MAKE A BOG GARDEN

A stand-alone bog garden
Built as an independent feature

↘A bog garden can be created by lining a hole with plastic, adding shingle for drainage, and installing a water feed to ensure that the soil is kept damp. To cut costs, use black plastic bags lapped over each other to line the hole.

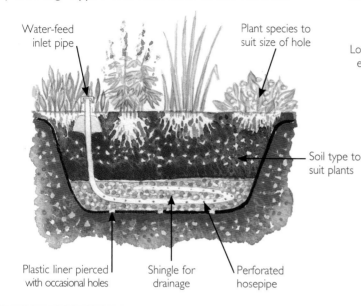

Water-feed inlet pipe

Plant species to suit size of hole

Soil type to suit plants

Plastic liner pierced with occasional holes

Shingle for drainage

Perforated hosepipe

A bog garden by a pond
Built to extend a pond's visual impact

↘A pondside bog garden is best built at the same time as the pond, using offcuts of liner. The bog garden will benefit from constant seepage from the pond, but you do have to ensure that it doesn't leach nutrients back into the water.

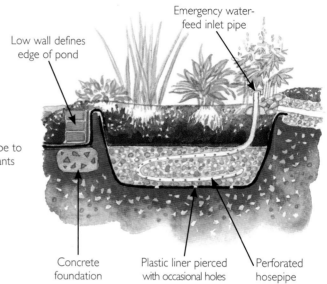

Emergency water-feed inlet pipe

Low wall defines edge of pond

Concrete foundation

Plastic liner pierced with occasional holes

Perforated hosepipe

BOG PLANTS

Bog plants – sometimes described by nurseries as 'moisture-loving plants' – positively enjoy being in damp soil, as long as the water in the soil is free-moving (see also pages 24–25). They will not be happy in soil that is waterlogged or in stagnant water. Many shallow-water marginal plants can also be grown successfully in bog gardens. Start with a small number of carefully researched plants, and see how it goes. Do not set the plants too deep, and make sure the area of bog neither dries out nor floods. Although bog plants require no more care than those in other parts of the garden, there are specific problems to watch out for:

- **Snail damage** – Large numbers of water snails can munch through new plants. Make sure there are suitable predators (see page 74) to limit the snail population.
- **Crown leaf rot** – If the crown of a new plant swiftly turns yellow, the likelihood is that it is unhappy with the depth of water. Try lifting the plant to slightly drier ground.
- **Insect pests** – Most insect pests can be controlled by rubbing them off with your fingers or by bringing in natural predators. Be very wary of using chemical controls because they might damage the wildlife.

CARE AND MAINTENANCE

- Clear out all plant debris from the bog garden at the start and finish of the season.
- If the water level rises to the point where it breaks the surface of the soil, you should spike the underlying butyl liner or plastic sheet so as to increase the drainage.
- If the bog garden dries out too quickly, then – by trial and error – either lower the edge of the pond slightly so as to increase the water run-off or direct additional water into the bog garden from house rainwater pipes.

A luscious mix of pond and bog plants that enjoy moist conditions.

Choosing water-garden plants

Are they difficult to grow?

You will need trees, shrubs and flowers to complement the pond and to enrich the wildlife habitat, bog plants for the damp ground around the water's edge, emergent or marginal plants for the shallows, floating or deep-water plants for a whole range of depths, and aquatic plants that may be completely or partially submerged. They are no harder to grow than any other garden plants, as long as you match them to the correct site.

PLANTING AIMS

Of course, you should choose plants that you like, but make sure you include ones that will oxygenate the water, as well as ones that will provide food and cover for all the wildlife in and around the pond (see also pages 10–11). When planting the areas around the water, choose plants both for their characteristics and for the fact that they will provide a habitat for all the creatures attracted by the water. You will not go far wrong if you plant a variety of the water plant types described opposite, plus a range of trees, grasses, shrubs and flowering plants in the immediate surrounds. Indirectly, all these plants will benefit the life in the pond.

CHARACTER AND HABIT

Do your research and read the labels, and try to imagine how the plants will look when they reach maturity. Will they be too tall or too spreading for the water garden? Will the roots perhaps damage the pond? Would it be better to go for smaller varieties? Are they going to be overtly beneficial for wildlife? Might a certain plant poison the water? Answering these questions should help you choose a good selection of attractive, but wildlife-friendly, plants.

BEST PLANTING POSITION

Plants only thrive when they are growing in conditions that suit their nature, so always read the labels before setting them in position. This is especially important with water plants that are depth-specific – some water plants will die if the water is too shallow or too deep for their liking.

There are irises to suit every growing situation – from slightly moist soil through to deep water, and from sunshine to shade. Iris pseudacorus *(Yellow Flag) loves wet conditions.*

PLANTING TIPS

- Be wary, in a pond that has been made with a butyl rubber liner (see pages 20–21), of growing plants that have sharp, pointed roots – such as some species of bamboo and couch grass.

- Make sure that no single tree, bush, grass or other plant around the pond overwhelms other species.

- Do your best, when planting in and around the pond, to use species that are common in your area.

- Underplant surrounding trees and shrubs with ground-cover plants.

TYPES OF WATER PLANT

Emergents or marginals

These are the plants that grow along the water's edge – in the shallows of slow-flowing streams, ponds and canals, for example. Although in general terms most plants are able to withstand short alternating periods of drought and flood, for emergents or marginals the depth of water is critical. Such plants are perfect for wildlife water gardens, where you are trying to encourage small creatures to take up home.

Waterside plants

This term covers just about any plant – tree, bush, shrub, flower, moss – that will in some way complement the water garden and is planted in ordinary soil around the edges.

Aquatics

Although there is some crossover between aquatics and floating plants (see below), the difference is that aquatics have root systems that dissolve and absorb nutrients. Some aquatics float, while others are partially or totally submerged. Aquatics clean up the water in two ways: they feed on all the 'rubbish' at the bottom of the pond, and they give off bubbles of oxygen. If you want high-quality water, which is good for wildlife, then you need aquatics.

Bog plants

These are plants that thrive in the wet soil of a bog garden and provide cover for frogs, newts, snakes, insects, mice and snails, among other creatures.

Floating or deep-water plants

These have leaves that float on the surface of the water, and roots that either trail in the water or anchor themselves into the mud at the bottom of the pond. The floating leaves and flowers provide cover for wildlife, and hold back the growth of algae. If you want to encourage a wide range of pondlife such as small fish, snails, newts and frogs, you need floating plants. Be aware that most floating plants are sensitive to water depth and water temperature.

PLANTING SCHEMES

Wildlife pond with small numbers of fish
- **Aquatics** – *Fontinalis antipyretica* (Willow Moss), *Potamogeton crispus* (Curled Pondweed)
- **Floating or deep-water plants** – *Aponogeton distachyos* (Cape Pondweed), *Myriophyllum aquaticum* (Parrot's Feather)
- **Emergents or marginals** – *Glyceria maxima* (Sweet Grass), *Iris versicolor* (Blue Flag)
- **Bog plants** – *Carex pendula* (Pendulous Sedge), *Miscanthus sinensis* 'Zebrinus' (Zebra Grass), *Osmunda regalis* (Royal Fern)
- **Waterside plants** – *Salix* spp. (Willows) (varieties native to your area)

Slow meandering meadow stream
- **Aquatics** – *Chara vulgaris* (Stonewort)
- **Floating or deep-water plants** – *Marsilea quadrifolia* (Water Clover), *Myriophyllum aquaticum* (Parrot's Feather)
- **Emergents or marginals** – *Glyceria maxima* (Sweet Grass), *Iris versicolor* (Blue Flag), *Ranunculus lingua* (Greater Spearwort)
- **Bog plants** – *Hosta* spp. (Hostas), *Iris* spp. (Irises)
- **Waterside plants** *Acer* spp. (Japanese Maples), *Cornus* spp. (Dogwoods), *Salix alba* subsp. *vitellina* 'Britzensis' (Scarlet Willow)

Japanese-style wildlife garden
- **Aquatics** – *Potamogeton crispus* (Curled Pondweed), *Ranunculus aquatilis* (Water Crowfoot)
- **Floating or deep-water plants** – *Azolla filiculoides* (Fairy Moss), *Nuphar japonica* (Japanese Pond Lily), *Salvinia auriculata* (Butterfly Fern)
- **Emergents or marginals** – *Calla palustris* (Bog Arum), *Iris laevigata* (Japanese Iris)
- **Bog plants** – *Athyrium filix-femina* (Lady Fern), *Cyperus alternifolius* (Umbrella Plant), *Eriophorum angustifolium* (Cotton Grass), *Osmunda regalis* (Royal Fern)
- **Waterside plants** – *Acer palmatum* (Japanese Maple), *Bambusa multiplex* 'Riviereorum' (Hedge Bamboo), *Tsuga canadensis* (Canadian Hemlock), *Salix babylonica* spp. (Weeping Willow)

Fish

Can I have fish in a small pond?

A well-balanced wildlife pond will support just about anything that swims, but the problem with fish is that they are very good at eating everything else. Research suggests that, if you do choose to have fish in a small pond, you will be limiting the numbers of other creatures. It is best to start by introducing a small number of native fish and see what happens before proceeding any further. Be ready to be ruthless if fish numbers outgrow the size of your pond.

FREQUENTLY ASKED QUESTIONS

- **What fish should I go for?** In the UK, minnows, sticklebacks, tench and rudd.

- **Will we be able to see the fish?** If the day is bright, you might catch sight of the fish flashing through the water, but for the most part small species like rudd and tench will be almost hidden from view.

- **How will species like tench and rudd benefit the pond?** They are bottom-feeders and as such will clean up all the debris and mess.

- **What do species like sticklebacks feed on?** Sticklebacks feed on small creatures such as water snails and worms.

- **We have a farm ditch that drains down into our water wildlife area – is this a problem?** Research suggests that part of the decrease in pondlife has to do with the fact that farmers have upped their livestock numbers, changed their dyke drainage for underground pipes, and increased their use of chemical sprays. This has not only directly resulted in an all-round drop in the numbers of wildlife creatures but, worse than that, toxic chemical residues are leaching into our gardens. The best advice is to dig out a sump at your end of the ditch and plant it with rushes, so you filter and break down some of the chemicals.

- **Are goldfish native?** While goldfish originated in Asia in the 1600s, they have been in the west for so long that they do very well in garden ponds.

- **Can we have big and small fish in the same pond?** You can, but remember that big, aggressive fish like tench are going to eat anything that comes their way. The bigger the pond, the lower the risk.

- **Should I feed my fish?** Be warned – if you make a habit of feeding your fish, the chances are they will become tame and easy prey for predators.

Make sure that the pond provides plenty of food and cover so that the fish are able to hold their own against potential predators.

CONTROLLING FISH NUMBERS

Fish are very good at eating and multiplying. You might think this is good – and it is – but the difficulty is that as the numbers of fish go up, the numbers of other creatures in and around the pond go down. Does this matter, though? The answer is yes, because there is a knock-on effect. Fewer water fleas might result in fewer amphibians, resulting in fewer snakes, resulting in fewer small birds, and so on. Too many fish will have a detrimental effect on all the creatures in the water garden, and far beyond. It is true that there are plenty of birds and mammals that love to feed on small fish, but in itself this natural culling may not be sufficient to keep your fish numbers in balance.

If you want to adopt the natural approach, then only introduce limited numbers of fish that are considered to be native to your area, and be ready to be ruthless if the fish population gets out of control.

Carassius auratus

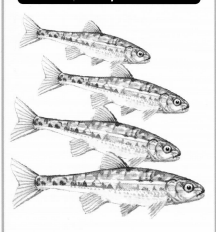

Goldfish

Reliable fish, good for ponds in a cold climate. Colours range from reddish-gold to creamy yellow. Grows up to 40 cm (16 in) long and lives for 19–25 years.

Avoid fancy breeds of goldfish because they are more expensive, need more space, and are liable to perish during a cold winter.

Phoxinus phoxinus

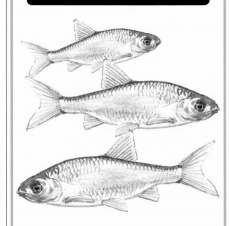

Minnow

Swift-swimming tiddler, good for small wildlife ponds. Colours range from pale orange to silvery red-brown. Grows up to 8 cm (3½ in) long and lives for 2–5 years.

Shoals of minnows look wonderful in ponds and streams, and are loved by small children.

Rutilus rutilus

Roach

Attractive, reliable, subtly coloured fish, good for large, muddy-bottomed wildlife ponds and lakes. Colours range from yellow-red to brown-gold. Grows up to 25 cm (10 in) long and lives for 5–8 years.

Roach will tolerate both clear and muddy water.

Scardinius erythrophthalmus

Rudd

Fat-bodied fish, suitable for both small and large ponds. Colours range from golden yellow to orange-red. Grows up to 30 cm (12 in) long and lives for 6–8 years.

Rudd will tolerate cloudy water, poor oxygen levels and big changes in temperature.

Tinca tinca

Tench

Reliable, rather shy but aggressive fish, which might well eat small fry and tadpoles. Colours range from green to a pale orange-gold. Grows up to 40 cm (16 in) long and lives for 10–12 years.

Tench are a good idea for a large wildlife pond, but a bad idea if you want ornamental fish.

CHILDREN AND FISH

Given a chance, most children will enjoy messing about in water – paddling, exploring, looking at insects, and of course catching fish. Encourage their watery activities by setting them up with a jar, a net and a notebook. Get them to look at the sludge, make a record of the various creatures, and generally take note of what is going on. They will have a great time, and who knows where these first splashings and sploshings might lead. Never forget, however, that water can be dangerous (see pages 14–15).

FISH PREDATORS

If you have established a really good wildlife pond, then you have to accept that it is an open door through which all manner of creatures will pass. Within the water garden, small fish will feed on insects, big fish will feed on small fish, big birds will feed on big fish, foxes will feed on birds, and so on. But do not worry – if you have set up the pond with plenty of planting for food and cover, your fish should be able to hold their own.

Amphibians

What type of creatures are they?

Frogs, toads and newts are all amphibians, meaning that their body temperature varies with their surroundings, they lay eggs en masse (called spawn) that develop into tadpoles, and they hibernate during the winter months. Where there is a likelihood that newts and frogs will be in competition, the newts will usually win out, so it is unlikely that you will have a community of frogs, toads and newts in the same pond.

Frogs produce masses of spawn because only a small proportion will survive to adulthood.

FROGS AND TOADS

Many species of frog and toad are in decline, possibly because of modern farming methods. To encourage frogs and toads, you need to build a good wildlife pond that is completely free of chemicals. Since they will return year after year to the same breeding ponds, it is possible to establish a breeding colony in your garden pond simply by bringing in spawn from one of the accredited conservation organizations.

Frogs and toads mostly eat insects, worms, slugs and snails, but they will, given the chance, eat just about anything from small mammals, birds and fish to each other, and even pet food. Frog and toad tadpoles eat plants and algae growing on the plants. The warmer the water in the pond, the faster will be the development from spawn to froglet or toadlet. Although frogs and toads are relatively safe from predators at the spawn stage, the moment they turn into tadpoles they become easy hunting for fish, birds, adult frogs and toads, snakes and many other waterside creatures.

NEWTS

Although at first glance newts look a bit lizard-like, they move slowly, prefer damp and shade rather than full sun, and have a smooth, velvety skin rather than scales. Newts eat worms, slugs, snails, insects, tadpoles, froglets and each other. In spring, newts head for the breeding ponds – the males first and then the females. By the time the females arrive, the males have developed their breeding characteristics – coloured crests and webbed toes. Newts lay their eggs in ones and twos until they have a clutch of about 300. Newt tadpoles eat bugs and insects.

Bufo bufo

Common Toad

Found in Europe, North Africa, the UK and some parts of the USA, but numbers have been decimated by pollution. Colours range from reddish brown to blackish brown. The female grows to a maximum adult length of about 13 cm (5 in), while males are smaller at about 7.5 cm (3 in). In spring, the female lays about 4,000 eggs in long ribbon-like strands.

Rana temporaria

Common Frog

Found in Europe and the UK, but numbers are declining. Colours range from muddy brown to yellow-red fawn. It grows to a maximum adult length of about 12 cm (4½ in). The female tends to have a brown-red belly; the male's is grey to whitish. Breeding takes place in spring. Frogs are known to favour certain ponds over others, and they sometimes return en masse to areas where the ponds have long gone. A healthy female will lay up to 2,000 eggs in large clusters of spawn, and the growth stages – spawn to tadpole to adult frog – take about three months. Given the right conditions, a frog will live for six or more years.

A male great crested newt, with the characteristic crest that runs from the head to the tail and on around the underside through to the back legs.

STUDYING AMPHIBIANS

A good way for children to study the spawn stage of frogs and toads is to keep a small amount of spawn in a jar of water, and then use a good-sized magnifying glass to focus in on the egg and post-egg stages. If you are patient, you will see all the developmental stages – the black blobs in the spawn moving, the tadpoles taking shape, the tails getting shorter, the growth of the legs, and the little froglet or toadlet hopping out onto dry land.

If you are keen to study the newts in your pond, take a torch and go down to the pond on a series of warm evenings in spring, and lie on your stomach with your face very close to the water. If you shine the light down through the water you might, if you are lucky, see newts at the breeding, egg-laying and tadpole stages. At breeding time, adult newts tend to show extra bright colours on their skin, such as much larger flashes of yellow and orange.

Triturus helveticus

Palmate Newt

Pale olive-brown to olive-green, with and without dark spots, very much like the common newt but without the spotting on the throat. The breeding male has a low, straight-topped crest running from neck to tail, 7.5–10 cm (3–4 in) long. On land, the female has a reddish stripe on the back; this can be seen in the breeding season from mid-spring to early summer, but is less obvious at other times.

Triturus cristatus

Great Crested Newt

Found in the UK and Europe, this newt is darkish black-brown with a yellow-orange underside and grows to 13–15 cm (5–6 in) long. The crest runs from head to tail on the back, round the tip of the tail and on the underside of the tail through to the back legs. There are 'source' ponds that have well-established colonies, where newts breed and disperse, and 'sink' ponds where they occasionally breed.

Triturus vulgaris

Common Newt

This newt is smooth-skinned and ranges from dark black-brown to yellow-orange fawn. It grows to a length of 7.5–10 cm (3–4 in). In the breeding season, the male develops wavy crest from neck to tail.

Dragonflies

How can I attract dragonflies?

An amazing fact about dragonflies is that, after spending two years or so living in the pond, and emerging as stunningly beautiful creatures, they live out their whole adult lives in a few weeks. During this time they mate and the breeding cycle recommences. Their main needs are clean water, a variety of water plants, and preferably an absence of fish. Big ponds mean lots of dragonflies – the more mud, plants and reeds the better.

BREEDING CYCLE

Dragonflies lay their eggs on the stems of water plants. The eggs turn into larval nymphs, and stay in the water feeding on pond debris and each other. After about two years, the nymph metamorphoses into an adult dragonfly. Having climbed out of the water along the stems of marginal plants and dried off their wings, the dragonflies take to the air and appear as the pretty flying insects we are so familiar with. Sadly, poor water quality in many rivers, streams and ponds has resulted in various species being threatened.

DRAGONFLIES AND FISH

Some adult dragonflies are able to catch small fish, but a high fish population in your pond will inevitably result in a low dragonfly population since the fish will eat the nymphs. If you want both fish and dragonflies, try putting a dam across the pond so that some part of the dragonfly population has a safe refuge.

COMMON DRAGONFLIES

Dragonflies are divided into two groups: 'hawkers', which fly backwards and forwards in search of prey, and 'darters', which make a swift dash or dart after their prey.

STUDYING DRAGONFLIES

A good way to study dragonflies is to pick a hot, still day in high summer, down beside a well-established pond – with a variety of refreshments, a notebook, binoculars and a good camera – and simply watch the water and wait patiently. If you want to go one step further, you can set yourself up in a hide and mount your camera on a tripod for even better results.

Aeshna juncea

Common Hawker

Widely distributed in the UK, but smaller than the Emperor, the male has blue spots on the body whereas the female is more green than blue. The adult male has a wingspan of 7.5–10 cm (3–4 in). It patrols the river bank in search of insect prey; the males sometimes cluster in large numbers.

Anax imperator

Emperor Dragonfly

This hawker is widely distributed in the UK, but numbers are declining. It has a brilliant blue/black-banded body, black markings on the wings, huge eyes, bristly legs, and a wingspan of 10–13 cm (4–5 in). The adult can reach flying speeds of 29–32 kph (18–20 mph). It eats flying insects and lays its eggs on the lower stems of emergent plants.

Libellula quadrimaculata

Four-spotted Chaser

Although this dragonfly is a darter, it has many hawking characteristics. The adult male has a golden-brown colour, a short body, and a wingspan of about 7.5 cm (3 in). The males will aggressively guard their own stretch of water.

Other pondlife

Take a magnifying glass to any well-established pond and you will see that every smear of mud, snip of plant and cup of water is teeming with wildlife. There are aquatic insects, such as the mayfly and caddis fly, as well as invertebrates (animals without a backbone), such as leeches, water stick insects, water snails and water boatmen. Even more types of creature are to be found living in and around streams and brooks.

What else lives in a pond?

STUDYING PONDLIFE

If you are looking for a fascinating year-round interest, get a scoop net, a sketch book, a diary, plenty of pencils, plenty of different-sized containers, a good pair of rubber boots, and a digital camera. You need to have a chair and table down by the pond, and a little shed or hide. Start by making regular visits and by recording observations in the diary.

Make sure there are several vantage points around the pond, so you can always see the water, plants and creatures to best effect.

Corixa spp.

Water Boatman

A brown-gold-black, beetle-like invertebrate that scuds about on the surface of pond water. It grows to a length of about 1 cm (½ in). These creatures look like little boats skimming across the water's surface. They are so buoyant that they hardly dent the surface tension of the water. They eat plant detritus and algae.

Lymnaea stagnalis

Great Pond Snail

A largish, brown-green snail, 2.5–5 cm (1–2 in) in length, which eats watery debris, fish waste and algae. There are many other types of still-water snail. If there is an imbalance in your pond and the numbers of snails get out of hand – to the point where the plants begin to suffer – lure them with floating cabbage leaves, and put them on the bird table.

Phryganis spp.

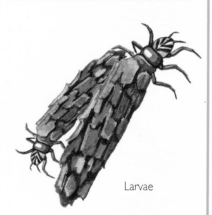

Larvae

Caddis Fly

Brown-grey in colour, the caddis fly spends most of its life in the water as a larva before emerging as a large, moth-like, flying insect. The larvae live at the bottom of the pond in little cases made from leaves, sticks and pond debris. The larvae are often used by fishermen to bait their hooks.

Water birds

Wildfowl, such as ducks, swans and geese, are web-footed birds that live on, in and near water. Ducks are the smallest of these, and therefore more likely to visit a pond in a country garden. Rails, such as coots and moorhens, are smallish, shy birds that live near slow-moving water – to attract them you could try creating large areas of bog garden near your pond. Herons may also visit if you have fish.

Keeping domestic geese will help to attract a wide variety of wild species to your pond.

POINTS OF INTEREST

- Ducks are born with feathers, and ducklings can be seen swimming soon after hatching.
- There are three groups of ducks: surface-feeding or dabblers, which feed in shallow water by dipping and dabbling; divers, which go to greater depths than the dabblers; and sawbills, which dive for plants and fish.
- Geese are generally bigger than ducks but smaller than swans, and have stout legs so that they can walk and graze on meadows and marshes.

Anas platyrhynchos

Mallard

The male has a breeding plumage of a dark green head, while the female has a brown head and a green flash on the wings. It is very common on ponds and lakes, and grows to about 55 cm (22 in) from bill to tail. It feeds by upending and surface dabbling and can take off into flight straight from the water. Mallards can become tame.

Anser albifrons

White-fronted Goose

Common on marshes and meadow ponds, this goose has a white blaze or line between the pink or orange bill and face, and grows up to 75 cm (2½ ft) long. It can be seen in large flocks in the UK, Europe, Russia and Canada. You might see one close at hand if your pond is in the country and close to marshes and water meadows.

Cygnus olor

Mute Swan

This swan has an orange-yellow bill with a black knob at the base. About 1.5 m (5 ft) long, it is bigger than *Cygnus columbianus* (Bewick's Swan; Tundra Swan; Whistling Swan). At a distance, it can be confused with *Cygnus cygnus* (Whooper Swan) since it has a similar body shape and feeds in open water. If your pond is near to fields and/or water meadows, you might have visiting swans. Some people keep domestic ducks and geese specifically to attract in wild species.

- Geese and swans are more likely to be seen in large country gardens than in small gardens.
- Rails prefer slow-moving water with plenty of reeds, and are characteristically shy. To see them, you will need to have large areas of swampy, marshy water and keep a careful lookout.
- Generally, rails feed on invertebrates, fruit, seedlings and some small tender plants.

HERONS

If you are one of those gardeners whose big pleasure in life is having a huge open pond stuffed with fish, then herons are going to be an annoyance, simply because they will be attracted by the easy eating. However, if you have a muddy-edged wildlife pond with a broad range of creatures – fish, frogs, newts and so on – and if the pond is generously planted with trees and shrubs all around it, then the creatures in the pond will at least have a fighting chance, and the heron will be presented with more of a challenge.

STUDYING WATER BIRDS

The easiest way to study water birds in your garden is simply to sit and watch them feeding, swimming, grooming and so on. The next step is to get a pair of binoculars, a digital camera with a good long-distance lens, and a diary or notebook in which to record your sightings. If you have a hide (see page 39) from which you can observe without being seen, so much the better, especially for the more timid rails.

While your water garden is getting established, a family of domestic ducks (here Muscovy ducks) can provide a huge amount of pleasure for you and your children.

Fulica atra

Coot

A duck-like bird with black plumage, a white shining bill that runs high up onto the forehead, and long legs that trail during flight. Coots are much more aggressive than moorhens, to the extent that they will actively attack to defend their territory.

Gallinula chloropus

Moorhen

This duck-like bird has black-brown plumage, green legs and a red bill. The name comes from the Old English word 'more' or 'moor', meaning boggy or swampy. It grows to about 30 cm (1 ft) long. The walking and swimming actions are both slow and jerky, as if the birds are being cautious.

About birds

What is so special about birds?

Birds are important simply in the sense that they are beautiful in their own right – what could be lovelier than the sight and sound of a blackbird in spring? Yet they are also a measure of the health of our gardens. If you have a variety of birds going about their normal business of feeding, fighting, nesting, breeding and bringing up their young, the likelihood is that everything in and around your garden is doing well.

THE GARDEN HABITAT

In the past, it was thought that birds were happiest in 'the wild countryside' and gardens were a kind of second best, but current research suggests that, in many ways, gardens are of primary importance. In the UK, Europe or the USA, many of the areas that we think of as being 'wild' – fields, meadows, farmland – are in fact areas that were once woodland. The pattern of our gardens, with trees and hedges all around, mixed planting, patches of overgrown weeds, compost heaps, rotting vegetation, vegetable gardens, ponds and bogs, buildings and so on, is more like the original natural woodland than modern farmland is.

So, when you plan and plant up your wildlife garden (see pages 36–37), you are, more by default than by design, creating areas that many birds regard as being wild and natural. Of course, you still will not attract birds that are entirely outside your region, but you will, if current surveys are anything to go by, attract around 25–40 different species.

It is also important to change your way of thinking, so that when you see your cabbages being attacked by greenfly, for example, you think of the greenfly not as pests but as food for birds and other wildlife. With this mindset, all the things that you once thought of being negative for your flower garden – weeds, flowers with dead heads, overgrown areas, piles of leaves, slugs and snails, ants, rotting fruit – you can now regard as positive for your bird garden.

SUPPLEMENTARY FEEDING

Feeders, bird tables and shop-bought bird food (see pages 38–39) are fine, and a good way of encouraging birds into your garden initially. Remember, however, that in the long term you should always be aiming to convert your garden into a 'natural' wildlife habitat with no need for such feeding. Over-generous supplementary feeding can also skew the population of some species at the expense of others.

POINTS TO CONSIDER

- The best way to attract birds is to create a large wildlife pond, which will bring in all the insects and other small creatures that birds like to eat.

- Cats are a nuisance, and you will have to do your best to keep them out (see pages 12–13).

- Small dogs are good – they might scare off a few birds, but they will also frighten cats (see pages 12–13).

- Research which birds are common in your area, and then encourage them by managing your planting so that there is a year-round supply of food – seeds, nuts, berries, fruit and insects (see pages 36–37).

- Plant trees and grasses that are local to your area.

- Increase the number of compost heaps, so as to encourage as many worms and insects as possible – all good food for birds.

Children are fascinated by nests and eggs, so it is essential to explain to them that they must only look from a distance and never try to handle a nest or its contents.

A blue tit (see page 48) searching for food, such as flies, bugs and other insects. Tits are also regular visitors to garden feeders.

This **Dendrocopos major** (*Great Spotted Woodpecker*) drums on a tree trunk with its bill to proclaim territorial rights.

A barn owl (see page 45) at dusk, poised and looking for the next meal – note the characteristic heart-shaped face.

A robin (see page 40) on the lookout for worms and bugs – this is one of the most common and familiar visitors to gardens.

Planning and planting the garden

Your garden must include a series of habitats, with each area providing a safe place for birds to feed, shelter and roost or nest. If you have mainly lawn, you will need to redesign the garden so that you have the largest possible pond, bog gardens around the pond, as many trees and shrubs as space allows, plenty of seed-producing plants, herbaceous borders and ground cover, with the lawn reduced to a path between the areas.

DESIGN CONSIDERATIONS

- **Wild areas** – Allow large areas of your garden to 'go wild' by minimizing lawns and holding back on tidiness (no clipping, deadheading or brushing). Plant a wildflower meadow, and set areas aside for weeds.
- **Food** – Plant as many berry-bearing species as possible, such as elder, hawthorn, honeysuckle, cotoneaster, pyracantha and yew (see below). Choose species that flower and fruit at different times.

- **Water** – Create the biggest possible pond, with related bog gardens and pools.
- **Nesting** – Provide as many nesting options as possible, including trees, shrubs, bushes, ground-cover plants and maybe a few nesting boxes.
- **Feeders** – If you choose to have supplementary feeders (not necessarily a good option – see page 34), make sure you site them so that cats cannot creep up unnoticed.

Shed or hide from which to study birds

Wood-chip paths

Fruit tree

Wildflowers and grasses

Big pond with island

Roses

Mixed hedge provides fruit and cover

Cotoneaster

Helianthus annuus (Sunflowers)

Lonicera (Honeysuckle)

Bog garden

Evergreens and shrubs

Mixed annuals

PLANTING FOR FOOD AND SHELTER

Across the various species, birds eat everything from seeds and fruits to aphids, beetles, flies, caterpillars and just about everything else that grows, buds, pupates, flies, crawls, slithers and swims. Therefore, to attract a wide variety of birds, you must plant a good range of trees, bushes, ground-cover plants, vegetables and grasses. These will provide much better natural food sources than supplementary shop-bought food on a bird table. When it comes to shelter and nesting sites, research suggests that one good-sized tree is worth any number of nesting boxes.

PLANTS FOR BIRDS

- *Alnus glutinosa* **(Alder)** – Good for boggy areas; provides shelter and food for birds that eat seeds.

- *Berberis* **spp. (Barberry)** – Produces vast numbers of flowers and berries that are good for both insects and birds; makes a good hedge for nesting.

- *Brassica oleracea* **(Cabbage)** – Attracts birds that feed on aphids, moths, butterflies and caterpillars.

- *Briza maxima* **(Quaker Grass)** – Attracts birds that feed on small seeds.

- *Buddleja alternifolia* **(Buddleia)** – Likes a sunny wall; the colour, smell and nectar attract butterflies and moths which in turn provide food for birds.

- *Cotoneaster* **spp. (Cotoneaster)** – Grows in almost any soil; provides food for birds that feed on berries.

Cotoneaster

- *Crataegus monogyna* **(Hawthorn)** – Grows in most soils and is good as a hedge; provides shelter and attracts birds that feed on berries, moths and caterpillars.

- *Helianthus annuus* **(Sunflower)** – Attracts birds that feed on large seeds.

- *Ilex aquifolium* **(Holly)** – Attracts birds that feed on berries.

Ilex aquifolium (Holly)

- *Limnanthes douglasii* **(Poached Egg Plant)** – Plant alongside poppies to provide a seed-rich meadow type environment for small birds.

- *Papaver commutatum* **(Poppy)** – Good for growing in areas of rough grass and meadow; the dead heads are packed full of seeds that will attract a whole range of small birds.

- *Prunus x domestica* **(Plum)** – Grows in well-drained ground; attracts birds that feed on fruits, aphids, moths, caterpillars, mites and flies.

Prunus x domestica (Plum)

- *Prunus cerasifera* **(Cherry Plum)** – Attracts moths, flies and aphids that in turn provide food for birds.

- *Rosa* **spp. (Roses)** – Attract birds that feed on aphids and rosehips.

- *Rubus fruticosus* **(Blackberry)** – Good for hedges and screening; provides shelter and food for birds that eat beetles, fruits and seeds.

- *Secale cereale* **(Rye)** – Attracts birds that feed on small seeds.

Buddleja alternifolia (Buddleia)

Boxes, tables, baths and hides

Are there any other ways to attract birds?

The best way to lure birds into your garden in the long term is to fill it with all the right plants (see pages 36–37). In the short term, however, you can attract them by providing instant feeding stations, nesting sites and a bath in which to have a good splash in clean water. You can either make these items yourself or buy them ready-made. An observation hide will enhance your enjoyment of your avian visitors.

NESTING BOXES

- **Chimney box** – With this type, the bigger the box the better; it is really good for owls and other large birds that might otherwise avoid garden sites.
- **Treecreeper box** – This is a good option for treecreepers and other birds that favour well-wooded sites, and it might also attract other beneficial creatures such as bats.
- **Tit box** – The size limits the box to small birds, the idea being that larger, more aggressive birds are kept out.
- **Dovecote** – A cote of the shape, size and character shown on page 43 provides a safe haven not only for doves but also for a wide variety of other birds.

Make sure, when you are choosing a nesting box, that the size and form suits your targeted birds.

HOW TO MAKE AN OPEN-FRONTED NESTING BOX

Some species of birds – such as robins, pied wagtails and spotted flycatchers – prefer to make their nests in a suitable crevice or cranny. For them, the open-fronted box is the best option. Do not worry about being too accurate with your measurements – after all, natural crevices are not perfectly shaped. The open design will allow you to swiftly inspect the contents – the mother, eggs and chicks, if you are lucky – without disturbing the birds. When choosing a site, opt for one that is hidden away in foliage, in a spot that is out of the prevailing wind, rain and direct sunlight.

Step-by-step procedure

1 Take all your wood – rot-resistant cedar is ideal – and saw it down to a thickness of about 1 cm (½ in).
2 Set the backboard, A, out with a ruler and square. Fix your compass to a radius of 3.5 cm (1½ in) and scribe out the shape of the half-circle details at the top and bottom. (Note that the stepped details are optional.)
3 Use a scroll saw to cut out the stepped half-circle details.
4 Use a drill to create fixing holes to a size that suits your needs.
5 Sand all the edges to a smooth square finish, and fix in place with glue and panel pins.
6 Colour the whole box with a watercolour wash, and follow this with a coat of exterior-grade water-based varnish if desired.

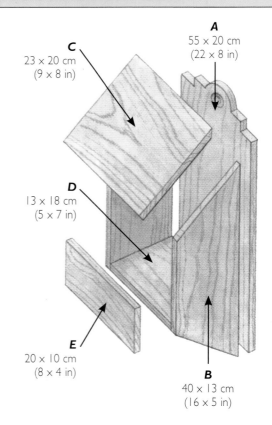

A
55 × 20 cm
(22 × 8 in)

C
23 × 20 cm
(9 × 8 in)

D
13 × 18 cm
(5 × 7 in)

E
20 × 10 cm
(8 × 4 in)

B
40 × 13 cm
(16 × 5 in)

Position your bird bath so that the birds have a clear all-round view, and make sure that it is always filled with clean water.

BIRD TABLES AND FEEDERS

There is a huge range of ready-made hanging feeders and tables on the market, but it is also possible to make your own if you have the time. You can quickly fill these with shop-bought food such as peanuts, mealworms and sunflower seeds, and there is no doubt that this easy food will be appreciated by some birds. A much better plan is to concentrate your main physical and monetary efforts on planting (see pages 36–37). In this way, you will be creating a long-term habitat with a consistent, sustainable source of natural food, and your feeders and table will become virtually redundant.

A home-made feeder designed to hold kitchen scraps.

BIRD BATHS

Traditional bird bath Make sure, when you are siting the bird bath, that you put it in a position where the birds have a good, all-round, clear view of things – so they can avoid the local cats.

Japanese hewn stone fountain Research suggests that a fountain of this character is a good option for birds, since cats stay away because they are wary about the moving water and the noise made by the hidden pump.

A traditional bird bath is both ornamental and practical

Water is a vital component of Japanese gardens, which aim to recreate nature in miniature

OBSERVATION HIDES

One of the best ways of enjoying a wildlife garden is to build a hide (see page 15) where you can tuck yourself away in order to observe creatures such as birds without any danger of being seen. It does not have to be fancy; just about anything will do – an old shed, a tent, a treehouse, a basic structure made of branches and an old tarpaulin – as long as it is dry, hidden away or camouflaged, and comfortable. The idea is that you can sit with a notepad and pencil, binoculars, a camera, perhaps even a novel, and your preferred refreshments, and then simply wait and watch.

Common garden birds

Which birds are most likely to appear?

Depending on where you live, but irrespective of the size of your garden, in many parts of Europe and the USA some of the most common birds you are likely to encounter are robins, sparrows, blackbirds and thrushes (although numbers have been declining in some regions in recent years). Apart from sparrows, these birds all produce beautiful song that can be enjoyed especially during the 'dawn chorus', for which you will have to get up early!

Erithacus rubecula

Adult

Robin

Size – 13–15 cm (5–6 in) long.

Appearance – A fat, round-looking bird with a characteristic red-orange face and breast, red-brown back and wings, olive-brown underparts and a black bill.

Habitat – A fixture in most British gardens, living on and around structures, houses, sheds and outhouses, and often also seen in hedges and bushes in parks and allotments. Very common in country orchards.

Feeding young

Food – Insects and larvae; robins often accompany gardeners when they are digging.

Nesting – Nests during spring in holes, nooks and crannies in sheds, outbuildings and trees, and normally has 2 broods per year.

Comments – Robins are more or less tame in most town gardens, to the extent that they will come to within touching distance; the disadvantage is that they often fall prey to cats. The call is a sharp 'tic-tic-tic-tic'. The similar species *Turdus migratorius* (American Robin) is common in gardens in the USA. Occasionally, migrant American robins are found in Europe and the UK.

Passer domesticus

House Sparrow

Size – 13–15 cm (5–6 in) long.

Appearance – Plumage is black, brown, white and grey, with the male having more complex patterns on and around the head and neck than the female, and a grey crown.

Habitat – Very common bird in British gardens, living on and around buildings and other structures such as sheds.

Food – Seeds left over from the harvest, and from common weeds.

Nesting – Breeds from spring to late summer, sometimes nesting in hedges and holes in trees, but prefers holes, nooks and crannies in buildings. The fledglings take aphids and other insects from their parents.

Comments – In the countryside, house sparrows prefer to build dome-topped nests in trees. Industrial farming and the increased use of chemicals has resulted in greatly reduced numbers. Even so, the house sparrow has been described as the most widely distributed wild bird on the planet.

Female

Male

Turdus merula

Male

Female

Blackbird

Size – 23–27 cm (9–11 in) long.

Appearance – The male has all black plumage and a yellow bill, while the female is more grey-brown with dappled grey-brown spots on the underparts. The female with her brown-black colour and blurred spots on the underparts can sometimes be mistaken for a thrush.

Habitat – Prefers open lowlands to dense woodland, but can be seen on woodland fringes as well as in gardens.

Food – Berries, worms and insects; will also eat kitchen scraps.

Nesting – Breeds from spring and has 2–3 clutches a year. Nests almost anywhere in hedges, in and on structures like sheds, in gutters and in roof eaves. Nest is built with grass leaves and feathers. Both parents feed the young for 2 weeks in the nest and 2 weeks out.

Comments – The moment you hear the beautiful 'pink-pink-pink' calll you will know that spring is just around the corner. The Blackbird is the national bird of Sweden.

Bowers and sheds make good nesting sites

Turdus viscivorus

Adult feeding on a worm

Mistle Thrush

Size – 23–27 cm (9–11 in) long.

Appearance – Plumage is black, brown, white and grey, with speckled brown on white underparts. Differs from the similar *Turdus philomelos* (Song Thrush) in that it has white underwings and white on the outer tail feathers.

Habitat – Gardens, parks and woodland; likes trees and hedges.

Food – Slugs, small snails, worms, berries and insects; breaks open snails by bashing them against a tree, stone or post.

Nesting – Breeds from spring to summer, nesting in hedges and low trees. The fledglings take aphids and insects from their parents; family groups tend to stay together in neighbouring trees, bushes and gardens.

Comments – A good bird to have in your garden if you enjoy growing vegetables and are troubled by slugs and snails.

ATTRACTING BIRDS

The best way of attracting birds to your garden is not to fill it full of peanut feeders, fat balls, nesting boxes and so on, but to increase your planting – lots more vegetables, berries, seeds, flowers and trees – so that you have a broad range of species that flower and fruit right across the seasons, and a good number of possible nesting sites. To put it another way, if you make sure that the food cupboard is well stocked, and there are plenty of nesting sites, then you can be sure that birds will come in. Do not forget, though, that you can only expect to attract bird species that are common to your area. You will not get reed warblers if you live in a high, dry area well away from water and reedbeds.

Once your planting is such that good numbers of birds come into your garden, you have to welcome all comers. Be aware of the fact that some large birds prey on smaller birds. So, for example, if your garden becomes a nesting place for small birds such as tits and finches, then larger birds such as crows and magpies will come in specifically to feed on them. This is natural.

Research suggests that our intensive agro-chemical farming methods are responsible for a 40 per cent drop in bird numbers, so the least we can do is give birds a home in our gardens. This may mean that you have to sacrifice a few seedlings and vegetables, but the rewards are well worth it.

Pigeons and doves

Are these birds unwanted pests?

The mention of pigeons and doves, which both belong to the family Columbidae, makes many vegetable growers nervous, because they will tuck into a variety of food crops. Despite that, the sight and sound of these birds cooing, gliding and swooping is magical. If you make sure that your wildlife garden contains plenty of seed- and berry-bearing plants and hedges, you will not need to worry so much about them eating your vegetables, if you grow them.

Columba palumbus

Woodpigeon

Size – 40–45 cm (16–18 in) long.

Appearance – Large, round, plump bird with green-blue-grey plumage with pink bloom on the breast, white on the neck, and a black band across the tail.

Habitat – Parks, gardens, farmland and woodland.

Food – Berries, acorns, fruit from orchards, a broad range of farm and garden crops, and seeds from common weeds; will also eat kitchen scraps.

Nesting – Breeds from spring to late summer, nesting in woodlands, gardens and parks – almost anywhere where there are good-sized trees – but will also nest in disused squirrel dreys, old barns and outhouses. The fledglings are nestbound for about 35 days.

Comments – Keep an eye on numbers, as woodpigeons can become a nuisance. If this happens, make contact with your local wildlife organizations and see what they advise. Farmers sometimes complain about these birds damaging their crops, but they may have helped to create the problem themselves by removing the hedges, bushes and trees that traditionally gave the pigeons their favoured berries, seeds and nuts.

Black feathers visible in flight

Adult at rest

You could use strings and nets to protect vegetable crops such as cabbages.

PROTECTING YOUR CROPS

The best wildlife-friendly way to protect your crops from woodpigeons is to plant more than you need, cover the plants with netting and fleece, make noise to frighten the birds away and attract in a neighbouring fox. That said, according to various wildlife interest groups in Europe, the UK and the USA, the best way of tackling the 'pigeon problem' is to get a good air rifle and shoot the birds for meat. This sounds drastic, but as the old adage says 'you love the birds you love to eat'.

Protect orchard crops by ringing them with other crops such as clover and kale.

Streptopelia decaocto

Adult at rest

Collared Dove

Size – 25–32 cm (10–13 in) long.

Appearance – Slim, broad-winged, long-tailed bird with pale sandy-buff plumage, black and white collar, black wingtips, and black-grey bill.

Habitat – Parks, gardens, farmland, woodland, towns and villages.

Food – Much the same as woodpigeons (see opposite).

Nesting – Nests in good-sized trees in evergreen woodlands, in gardens and parks, in old barns and outhouses, in sheds near chicken runs – almost anywhere where there is food and shelter.

Comments – As with woodpigeons, keep an eye on numbers, as collared doves can become a nuisance.

KEEPING DOVES AND PIGEONS

Nothing evokes the 'cottage garden' quite as well as a dovecote or pigeon loft. The huge traditional dovecote-cum-loft shown below is not only an attractive garden structure in its own right, but also provides a functional way of controlling bird numbers. It is beautifully simple – the pigeons and doves eat their fill in the surrounding hedgerows and fields, and then you step in and cull them for food. In this way, the birds get to live out their lives, you get to see flocks of birds variously swooping, circling and coming in to roost, and at the end you become a predator. Do not worry if you have gone to the trouble of building a loft or cote only to find that the birds have flown, since the structure will eventually give shelter to other wildlife such as owls, squirrels, mice, bats, moths and other insects. As for the question of whether or not we should be culling wild country pigeons for food, there are hundreds of bird-loving groups throughout the world that think that it is a good, responsible answer to the problem of pigeon over-population.

In times past, 'troublesome' pigeons and doves were given shelter and then culled for food.

Make sure, if you are giving a home to doves and pigeons, that it is high up above the ground and well away from cats.

Less common garden birds

If you live in a countryside property complete with tumbledown outbuildings, large ponds, streams or a river nearby, lots of old trees, and well-established old planting, you will see all the usual birds that are local to your area, plus slightly more exotic delights such as kingfishers, cuckoos, woodpeckers and owls, if you are fortunate. These unusual species are often favourites with children and, if you keep your garden chemical-free, the birds should be happy to visit it.

Which birds enjoy a rural setting?

Alcedo atthis

Kingfisher (UK) River Kingfisher (USA)

Size – 13–18 cm (5–7 in) long.

Appearance – Has orange plumage on the chest and iridescent blue-green on the back, short wings and a long, dagger-like bill.

Habitat – Slow-moving water, rivers, canals, lakes, meandering streams and mill ponds.

Food – Small fish and water creatures.

Nesting – Nests in holes and tunnels dug into a muddy riverbank.

Comments – Very striking bird, best seen when diving into the water to catch fish, and/or when perched and in the act of killing and swallowing a small fish.

Adult with its catch   *Adult in flight*

Nest tunnelled into riverbank

Cuculus canorus

Cuckoo

Size – 30–35 cm (12–14 in) long.

Appearance – Plumage is brown to grey-black with reddish orange on the top, with greyish head and white tips to the tail; the young female is sometimes a distinctive reddish brown.

Habitat – Old structures, rocky ledges, woodland, parks and meadows.

Food – Insects, especially caterpillars.

Nesting – The female lays her 20 or so eggs in the nests of other insect-eating birds. The hatchlings make room by pushing out some, or all, of the host eggs.

Comments – At first glance, the cuckoo can sometimes be mistaken for a bird of prey, such as a hawk; the identifying characteristics are the straight beak, rounded tail and distinctive 'cuckoo' call in spring.

Dunnock feeding cuckoo chick

Young adult

Picus viridis

Green Woodpecker

Size – 27–32 cm (11–13 in) long.

Appearance – Large-looking bird, with overall green-yellow plumage, and bright red on the forehead and around the black-ringed eyes. The rump is yellow. The male has a red cheek patch.

Habitat – Woodland where there is a mix of young trees and old trees with overgrown woody trunks.

Food – Insects and larvae, such as ants and grubs, either found on the ground or in crannies in the bark of trees.

Characteristic yellow rump is visible in flight

Male

Female

Nesting – Nests in holes in trees, either a hole it has found or one it has excavated.

Comments – It takes a pair of woodpeckers about 30 days to cut a hole in the trunk of a tree. Their sharp beaks make a rat-a-tat drumming sound, a bit like a stick on hollow wood. They have specially adapted claws that allow them to brace their tails against the tree trunk. While Green Woodpeckers do drum, they are not such persistent drummers as other woodpecker species.

Tyto alba

Barn Owl

Size – 30–35 cm (12–14 in) long.

Appearance – One of the smallest owls, it has gold-brown-buff-white plumage, with white on the underside, and a distinctive, heart-shaped, white face.

Habitat – Towns, villages and anywhere where there are buildings with open vents, lofts, windows, nooks and crannies.

Food – Small birds and mammals, such as rats, mice and voles.

Nesting – Nests high up in buildings in holes and lofts.

Comments – If you want a wildlife garden but are not so keen on rats and mice, then owls are good predators to encourage. Owl nesting boxes are a good option, but a hollow tree or an open hole high up in the gable end of a building would be better. If you are inviting in owls to feed upon mice and rats, you must not use rat poison or anything else that might indirectly harm the owl. In many areas, they are protected by law.

Barn owl looking for food

Barn owls eat wood mice

OTHER LESS COMMON BIRDS

- *Accipiter nisus* (**Sparrowhawk**) – Reddish brown bird of prey with short wings, long tail, yellow eyes, and huge, needle-sharp talons; it hovers and then swiftly darts down on its prey.
- *Luscinia megarhynchos* (**Nightingale**) – Usually heard before it is seen, this sweet-singing high-flyer is reddish chestnut-brown with cream-buff underparts.
- *Pica pica* (**Magpie**) – Has a black head and black-green-purple tail with dramatic bars and flashes of white on the front, underside and wings; it eats eggs and young from other nests.
- *Vanellus vanellus* (**Lapwing**) – Has black-green-black plumage with an orange undertail, white underparts and a distinctive head crest.

Swifts, martins and swallows

These delightful migrant birds appear in the UK in spring and summer to breed, and then fly south again in the autumn to overwinter in warmer climes. They are known to eat, sleep, drink, wash and even mate in flight, but they do all land to collect nesting materials, to nest and to bring up their young. Swallows and martins can often be seen in autumn gathering in numbers on telegraph wires before migrating.

Do they ever land on the ground?

NESTING SITES

While it is fair to say that few birds spend more time in the air than swifts, martins and swallows, and although it is true that they can do just about everything in flight – feed, eat, sleep and mate – they do of course alight to nest and to feed their young. The swift favours nesting in holes in cliffs and buildings, the swallow creates a cup-shaped nest high under the eaves of buildings, and the martin builds its nest in cliffs and rooftops. Swallows will often return to the same nesting area year after year.

A hungry brood of swallows in a characteristic, cup-shaped nest.

Apus apus

Swift (UK) Chimney Swift (USA)

Size – 15–18 cm (6–7 in) long.

Appearance – Has dark blue-brown plumage with sickle-shaped wings and a short forked tail.

Habitat – Villages and towns.

Food – Insects eaten while on the wing; the wide-gaping mouth scoops up high-flying insects by means of a specially adapted, funnel-shaped fringe of bristles that ring the face.

Nesting – Nests on buildings (in holes, on ledges and high up under overhanging eaves) and in holes in cliffs, using the same nest for several years in a row. Once a year, lays a clutch of 2–3 eggs. The parents store up food in large throat pouches, and then feed the young with small pellets – a mix of insects and saliva. Having stayed in the nest for about 40 days, the young fly away, never to return.

Comments – The swift spends most of its life in the air. They winter in Africa, arrive in countries like the UK and USA in spring, and leave in late summer.

Feeding in flight

Delichon urbica

House Martin (UK)
Common House Martin (USA)

Size – 10–13 cm (4–5 in) long.

Appearance – Has blue-black-brown upper parts and white underside, and appears in flight to have a white bar across the width of the lower back.

Habitat – Can be seen in towns, but prefers villages and open countryside.

Food – Insects eaten while on the wing.

Nesting – Usually builds its nest on the outside of a building in a sheltered spot under the eaves. There may be 2–3 broods of 4–5 young each throughout the summer. While returning house martins do sometimes come back to the same site and even to the same nest, it is also true to say that a single nest might, in any one year, be used by a number of different migrants.

Comments – Traditionally, it was thought to be a good omen to have house martins nesting under your house eaves – a sign that the household was content, lucky and long-lived. Summer visitors.

Viewed from above and below

Hirundo rustica

Male in flight

Adult feeding young

Swallow (UK) Barn Swallow (USA)

Size – 15–21 cm (6–8½ in) long.

Appearance – Blue-black on the head and back, and white on the underside, with red-russet details around the face and throat. In flight, depending upon the manoeuvre, the tail feathers are seen as either a long fork or two parallel feathers.

Habitat – Just about everywhere, but they seem to prefer villages, open countryside and farm buildings near slow-moving water.

Food – Insects eaten while on the wing.

Nesting – Nests in cup-shaped nests high up, usually inside buildings on roof beams or ledges. Raises 2–3 broods a year.

Comments – One of the few birds that regularly inhabits buildings. Summer visitors from Africa.

The tit family

The word 'tit' is derived from the **Old English** word 'tite', meaning very small, minute or smallest. In terms of body size – forgetting tail feathers – the long-tailed tit is one of the world's smallest birds. The tit family comprises around a dozen species, four of which are common in British gardens. Tits tend to go around in 'gangs', and are incredibly agile, perching effortlessly on tree branches and hanging feeders.

Aegithalos caudatus

Long-tailed Tit

Size – 13–15 cm (5–6 in) long.

Appearance – Has a black head with a white crown, and pinky-buff underparts. The tail feathers make up over half the total length, so the body length may be only 6 cm (2½ in).

Habitat – Woodland, farmland, hedges and gardens; particularly likes untidy, overgrown gardens and thick undergrowth.

Food – Insects, buds and seeds.

Nesting – Builds an enclosed, oval-shaped, bag-like nest using scraps and wisps of moss, hair, feathers and cobwebs, sited anywhere from a sheltered spot low down beside a tree trunk to a fork in a scrubby bush.

Comments – Nest-building is a joint effort with the males doing all the fetching and carrying of materials, and the females doing the more intricate construction.

Adult feeding its young

Characteristic long tail

Parus caeruleus

Blue Tit

Size – 10–13 cm (4–5 in) long.

Appearance – Has blue-green upper parts, yellow underparts, a blue crown and a white face.

Habitat – Woodland and wooded gardens.

Food – Insects, grubs and larvae; also likes supplementary food such as seeds, nuts, fruit and kitchen scraps.

Nesting – Nests in holes in trees and in nesting boxes.

Comments – Distinctive little bird that is a welcome addition to any garden.

Distinctive, chubby, round shape

Blue tits love fat balls

Parus ater

Coal Tit

Size – 10–13 cm (4–5 in) long.

Appearance – Has a black head with white on the neck and blue-buff underparts. While the young birds are generally duller than the adults, they do have small white/yellow-tinged patches on the nape of the neck and the cheeks.

Habitat – Woodland and overgrown wooded gardens, but prefers conifer woods.

Food – Insects found under the bark of trees; will also eat supplementary food such as fruit and nuts.

Nesting – Nests in holes in trees, nesting boxes, mouseholes, between the roots of trees – almost anywhere that is at about 1 m (3½ ft) or so from the ground.

Comments – Small, hardy bird that does well, even in harsh winters, by feeding on insects found in the crevices beneath tree bark, by searching around under leafmould, and by generally scratching around. It will feed at treetop level, on the ground, and all places in between. If you want to attract coal tits, build log piles in various corners of the garden.

Adult

Searching for insects

Parus major

Great Tit (UK)
Chickadee, Titmouse (USA)

Size – 13–15 cm (5–6 in) long.

Appearance – Has bluish green plumage with patches of green on the upper parts, a yellow belly, and white outer tail feathers.

Habitat – Woodland and wooded gardens.

Food – Insects, caterpillars and larvae; will also eat supplementary food such as nuts, seeds and kitchen scraps.

Nesting – Nests in holes in trees, cracks and crannies in old buildings, and in boxes (with holes about 6 mm/1¼ in across).

Comments – The biggest and noisiest member of the tit family.

Adult

Feeding young

OTHER TITS

- *Parus cristatus* (**Crested Tit**) – Has a pointed, black and white crest and favours pine forests.
- *Parus montanus* (**Willow Tit**) – Has a matt-black crown and favours wooded margins and hedges.
- *Parus palustris* (**Marsh Tit**) – Has a glossy black crown and pale white-grey wing patches, and prefers hedges, woodland and scrubby wasteland.

Finches

Which are the commonest finches?

Finches are 'passerines', meaning song or perching birds. Characteristically, they are small to medium in size, have short, stubby beaks and 12 tail feathers, build enclosed, basket-shaped nests, and sing well. Finches are common and widespread right across Europe and the USA. In the UK, the ones you are most likely to encounter in your wildlife garden are chaffinches, bullfinches, goldfinches and greenfinches, but if you live in a rural area you may see more.

Carduelis carduelis

Goldfinch

Size – 10–13 cm (4–5 in) long.

Appearance – The sexes are broadly similar with blue-black on the head, a red and white face, yellow bars across the wings, and brown-grey on the underparts.

Habitat – Just about everywhere from woodland, overgrown gardens and hedges to farmland, orchards and parks.

Food – Seeds, grain, nuts, fruit and young buds; will also eat kitchen scraps, but is not keen on nuts.

Characteristic cup-shaped nest

Nesting – Builds a cup-shaped nest from twigs, stems, moss, lichen, feathers and other soft materials, usually in the lower branches of a small tree or in bushes.

Comments – Its distinctive, bright red face makes it easy to recognize. The related species *Carduelis tristis* (American Goldfinch) is a familar garden visitor in the USA.

Adult – note the broad yellow bars on the wings when in flight

---

Fringilla coelebs

Chaffinch

Size – 13–15 cm (5–6 in) long.

Appearance – Has a blue-grey head with pink-brown on the shoulders, white bars on the wings, and pink-brown underparts. The female has much the same markings as the male, but the colours look more washed out.

Habitat – Farmland, hedges, orchards, open spreads of trees and overgrown gardens.

Food – Seeds, grains and nuts; will also eat kitchen scraps.

Nesting – Nests in trees and bushes in scrubland, in overgrown gardens, and on the edges of woodland – builds a cup-shaped nest using a carefully woven mix of grass, bark, hair, feathers and wool. A healthy female lays two clutches of eggs between spring and summer. From one bird to another, the eggs vary in colour from red-brown through grey-blue to grey-red.

Female

Male

Comments – Research suggests that in a good year there will be 6–7 million pairs in the UK. The chaffinch has a characteristic, low-slung, pot-bellied shape that makes it relatively easy to recognize.

Pyrrhula pyrrhula

Bullfinch (UK) Eurasian Bullfinch (USA)

Size – 13–17 cm (5–6½ in) long.

Appearance – Has a blue-black head, a white bar on blue-black wings, and red neck and underparts. The female is a paler pink version of the male.

Habitat – Although it is widespread in parks, gardens, farmland, edges of woods and orchards, it seems to have a preference for conifers and dense undergrowth on the edge of clearings.

Food – Seeds, fruit, berries and young buds.

Nesting – Generally builds a cup-shaped nest in lower branches close to the trunk high up, but they sometimes settle for building a flat, almost plate-like, mess of a nest. The nest is made from a mix of twigs, moss, leaves, hair and down.

Comments – Bullfinches can be a real problem in orchards and fruit farms, and just about anywhere where there are delicate buds. If you are troubled by bullfinches eating your orchard buds, then a good solution is to ring the orchard with crab apple trees.

Male

Female

Carduelis psaltria *(Lesser Goldfinch) is native to the Southwest of the USA. Here a male is perched so as to take best advantage of the early morning sun.*

OTHER FINCHES

- *Carduelis cannabina* **(Linnet)** – Has a red patch on the forehead, red breast and a chestnut-brown body, with white edges to the wings; it favours open farmland where there are hedges and dense scrubland with gorse and bramble.
- *Carduelis flammea* **(Redpoll)** – Has a red forehead, pink-brown back and pink breast; it favours woodland, conifers and densely planted gardens.
- *Carduelis flavirostris* **(Twite)** – Is streaky pink-brown, with a bright patch of pink down the upper back, and has a bright yellow bill in the summer; it favours open ground, coastal areas and moorland.
- *Carduelis chloris* **(Greenfinch)** – Is yellow-green in colour with a pink bill; it favours woodland, dense bushes and gardens.
- *Carduelis spinus* **(Siskin)** – Has a black crown with distinctive bright yellow-green body and wings, with yellow bars on the wings; it favours conifer forests.
- *Coccothraustes coccothraustes* **(Hawfinch)** – Has a light nut-brown body with white bars on the wings, and a large head with a large strong bill; it favours sheltered woodland and orchards.

About mammals and reptiles

Which animals might come to a garden?

A mammal is a warm-blooded animal that has fur on its skin, gives birth to living young and feeds its young with milk. A reptile is a cold-blooded, usually egg-laying, vertebrate with a skeleton and a body covered with scales and/or plates. If you are lucky, you will be visited by reptiles such as snakes, lizards and slow worms, and mammals such as mice, bats, moles, voles, hedgehogs, squirrels, rabbits and foxes.

MAMMALS AND REPTILES IN THE GARDEN

Much depends upon the size of your garden and where you live, but mammals and reptiles are only going to visit if you ensure that they have just the right shelter and food. Some of these animals will only be night-time visitors, and/or just travelling through, so they will not be wanting to set up a permanent home; but they will all be seeking food. Mice eat insects and spiders; hedgehogs eat worms, slugs and small animals; bats eat flying insects; badgers eat roots, worms and small mammals; foxes eat birds, small animals and insects; rats eat whatever is on offer; rabbits eat grass; and snakes eat small animals and insects. If your patch provides them with their needs, they will most certainly visit and might possibly stay.

THE GARDEN HABITAT

You need to think of your garden as one big mammal and reptile refuge, and then shape it up and stock it accordingly. Start with the pond (see pages 18–21) and all the minute creatures that live near it, and then work up. You should plan to have bog gardens (see pages 22–23) around the pond, lots of ground cover, several compost heaps, one or two left-alone areas for weeds, lots of rotting logs, long grass, larger bushes and shrubs, as many trees as the size of your garden allows, and a small shed, shelter or hide (see page 39) that is tucked quietly away so that you can watch the show. The larger animals will not all rush in, because the smaller creatures that they feed on need to establish themselves first, but if you are patient and keep things going for a year or two your garden will become a wildlife haven.

NATURE 'RED IN TOOTH AND CLAW'

It is sometimes very difficult to love wildlife in the raw. For example, once I was sitting with my binoculars quietly watching a family of five or so baby rabbits playing chasing games in the late-afternoon sun – they seemed to be having fun, just like puppies – when all of a sudden a fox appeared, and before long two of the rabbits were dead. Nature can appear difficult at times, but 'kill or be killed' is just the way of it. Every creature must eat to survive. You will have to accept this harsh fact if you are to become a wildlife watcher.

POINTS TO CONSIDER

- If your garden is too small for a pond you could increase the size of the bog garden and make sure that there are bowls and trays of water.

- Make sure that your shed, shelter or hide is hidden away and yet positioned so that you can see the action.

- You cannot do much about cats hunting in your garden, other than to make sure that there is good ground cover and plenty of structures, so that wild creatures have places to hide.

- Research suggests that long grass and trees attract a whole host of creatures.

A young hedgehog (see page 60) wondering how best to tackle this tasty handout.

GARDEN MAMMALS

A grey squirrel (see page 59) has smooth ears and a characteristic slightly grizzled tail. It buries food items for later retrieval.

A young rabbit (see page 58) that has been startled and is ready to bolt. It is interesting to note that rabbits will, especially when food is short, eat their own droppings.

A brown rat (see page 59) searching for insects and grubs. Note the short, fat tail.

A pair of fox cubs at play in the undergrowth. Note the characteristic pricked-up ears and the sharply staring, attentive eyes.

A house mouse (see page 58) busy eating scraps. House mice have long been happy to share both our food and our homes.

Planning and planting the garden

How can I attract mammals and reptiles?

You need to establish a sound bird garden (see pages 36–37), including a series of habitats such as bog gardens, as many trees and shrubs as the space allows, plenty of flowering, seed-producing plants, and lots of herbaceous borders and ground cover. Then you need to go one step further and make sure that your garden is also suitable for the range of mammals and reptiles that are local to your area.

DESIGN CONSIDERATIONS

- **Wild areas** – Allow large areas of your garden to 'go wild' by including as many overgrown areas as possible. Plant a wildflower meadow, and set areas aside for weeds. Reduce your areas of mown lawn.
- **Food** – Plant as many berry-bearing species as possible, to bring in birds and the animals that eat birds. Plant dense borders and heap up piles of dead leaves so as to encourage slugs and insects that will in turn become food for animals such as mice and bats. Plant as many trees as possible. Build more compost heaps for worms that in turn will become food for both reptiles and mammals.

- **Water** – Create the biggest possible pond, with related bog gardens and pools.
- **Shelter** – Build log piles to give homes to small mammals and reptiles. Make underground tunnels for badgers, foxes and rabbits. Animals like mice, hedgehogs and snakes also live underground, so dig a shallow hole, fill it with dry leaves, cover it over with a box topped with a sheet of glass and more leaves, and then simply leave it and see what moves in. You could also nail a wooden box under your roof eaves, or in a tree, and then wait; some creature will move in – perhaps even a bat.

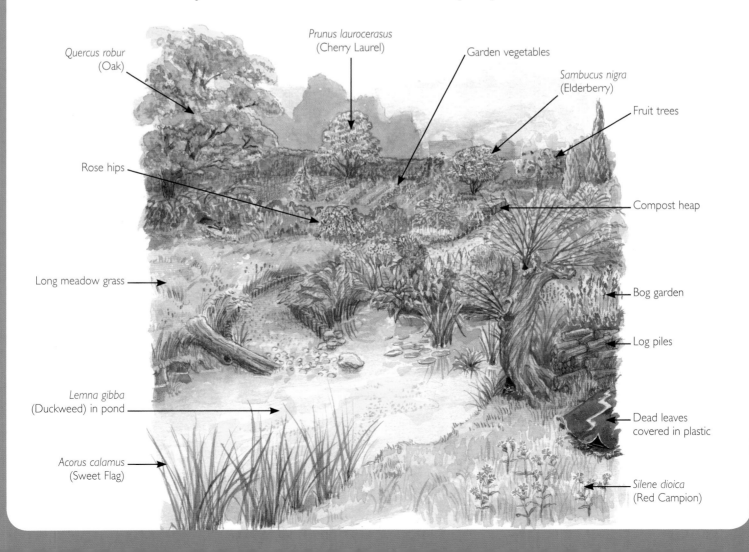

Quercus robur (Oak)

Prunus laurocerasus (Cherry Laurel)

Garden vegetables

Sambucus nigra (Elderberry)

Fruit trees

Rose hips

Compost heap

Long meadow grass

Bog garden

Log piles

Lemna gibba (Duckweed) in pond

Dead leaves covered in plastic

Acorus calamus (Sweet Flag)

Silene dioica (Red Campion)

THINKING ABOUT THE OPTIONS

The truth is, and this has to be faced, that when it comes to garden design wildlife prefers all the things that we traditionally have thought of as being not so good. Wildlife prefers long grass to short, scruffy areas to neat and swept, rotting wood to treated wood, overgrown inaccessible areas to patios and paths, holes and muddy areas to clean and dry, and so on. This is no problem if you are going to plant the garden, ring it with a tall wall and vanish from the scene, but it is not so easy if you also want to share the garden. The best way forward if you want a wildlife garden is to look at the total area, decide how little you want to 'tame', and then set about letting the majority go back to nature.

Think long and hard about such questions as whether a pond will be dangerous for children, whether cats will kill birds, whether mice will get into the house, whether snakes will eat birds, and so on. These are all important issues that need to be carefully considered in the context of your own particular house, garden and family set-up.

PLANTS FOR MAMMALS AND REPTILES

The following list of plants is intended both to feed the mammals and reptiles directly with roots, shoots and fruits, and to feed the insects and bugs that will become food for the mammals and reptiles. Long grass attracts insects, and garden vegetables also draw in insects, birds and small mammals.

- *Acorus calamus* (**Sweet Flag**) – Planted around the pond margins, this attracts slugs and insects.

- *Angelica sylvestris* (**Angelica**) – Attracts butterflies and other insects.

- *Castanea sativa* (**Sweet Chestnut**) – The nuts are attractive to mammals, including squirrels.

- *Fagus sylvatica* (**Beech**) – Produces lots of beech nuts that are very rich in edible oils; these are eaten by squirrels, rabbits, birds and small mammals.

- *Juglans regia* (**Walnut**) – The nuts attract squirrels and mice.

- *Lemna gibba* (**Duckweed**) – This floating plant attracts a wide range of snails and insects.

- *Lythrum salicaria* (**Purple Loosestrife**) – Attracts insects.

- *Prunus laurocerasus* (**Cherry Laurel**) – Provides food for beetles, bugs and butterflies.

- *Quercus robur* (**Oak**) – Acorns attract squirrels and badgers.

- *Sambucus nigra* (**Elderberry**) – Produces lots of berries and pips that are eaten by birds and small mammals.

- *Silene dioica* (**Red Campion**) – Brings in a range of insects.

Insects do best when there is plenty of good ground cover such as long grass and clumped plants.

Make sure there are plenty of berries and nuts being produced in your garden to attract mammals and reptiles.

Acorns

Beech nuts

Elderberries

Chestnuts

Angelica sylvestris (*Angelica*) attracts butterflies and insects that in turn attract birds, small mammals and reptiles to the garden.

Providing food

Many mammals and reptiles eat plant and animal material, so the best advice is include plants they can eat directly as well as ones that attract creatures they can eat. For example, sunflower seeds are eaten by insects, birds and small mammals, and these are in turn eaten by larger animals. You should always take great care when providing any supplementary food items such as kitchen scraps.

Should I put food out?

You may have put seeds and nuts out for the birds, but who can blame this grey squirrel for coming in for a feed?

Remember that your shop-bought bird food will attract in all kinds of other wild creatures such as this wood mouse.

SUPPLEMENTARY FEEDING

The rule of thumb here has got to be restraint and high quality or nothing at all. Hedgehogs might like drinking milk that you put out for them, and you could buy in worms, maggots, nuts or seeds, but each action on your part might have adverse effects. The seeds and nuts will have been shipped from foreign countries, the maggots will have been bred using fossil-fuel heat, and the super-abundance of nuts might encourage one bird or mammal to the detriment of another, and so on. You must be aware that, if you do decide to put out stale bread for pigeons, or scraps of meat for your friendly fox, you might be doing more harm than good. For example, if you put out regular supplies of nuts for a certain animal, and that animal comes to depend on your handouts – perhaps even holds back on its hibernation plans, or does not put by a cache of food for the winter – what happens to that animal if you decide to go off on a long holiday? What if your handouts consist mainly of low-quality white bread that swells up to twice its size in the animal's stomach?

The best advice is to restrict supplementary food to household food that would otherwise go to waste – scraps of fat, bread, cake, fruit and so on. Put all your potato peelings and outer leaves of vegetables on the compost heap. In this way, you will indirectly be giving supplementary food in the form of slugs, worms and all the beetles and bugs that live on, in or near the compost heap. Then direct all your efforts into creating a wildlife garden that is stuffed with super-food plants.

This Castanea sativa *(Sweet Chestnut) tree will provide food for mammals for a century or more.*

Plant a grass like Miscanthus sinensis *(Zebrinus) and you will be providing home and food for slugs, worms, mammals and reptiles.*

WHAT DO MAMMALS EAT?

- *Clethrionomys glareolus* **(Bank Vole)** – Small seeds, bulbs, shoots, roots, flowers and woody material.

- *Erinaceus europaea* **(Hedgehog)** – Insects, beetles, bugs, slugs, snails and small mammals.

- *Meles meles* **(Badger)** – Roots, shoots, bulbs, worms and small mammals, plus any dead animals that it comes across.

- *Microtus arvalis* **(Common Vole)** – Roots, grasses and small seeds.

- *Mus musculus* **(House Mouse)** – Scraps and anything else that looks tasty – fat, soap, candles.

- *Mustela nivalis* **(Weasel)** – Small birds and mammals.

- *Oryctolagus cuniculus* **(Rabbit)** – Seeds, grass, garden vegetables, tree bark and orchard crops.

- *Pipistrellus pipistrellus* **(Common Pipistrelle Bat)** – Flies, moths and most flying insects.

- *Rattus norvegicus* **(Brown Rat)** – Roots, shoots and small mammals.

- *Sciurus carolinensis* **(Grey Squirrel)** – Insects, beetles, bugs, roots, shoots, seeds and nuts.

- *Sciurus vulgaris* **(Red Squirrel)** – Roots, shoots, seeds, nuts and chestnuts.

- *Sorex araneus* **(Common Shrew)** – Insects, beetles, bugs, grasshoppers, slugs and carrion.

- *Sorex minutus* **(Pigmy Shrew)** – Beetles, insects, grubs, bugs and almost any animal material.

- *Talpa europaea* **(Mole)** – Beetles, bugs, insects and worms.

- *Vulpes vulpes* **(Red Fox)** – Insects, beetles, bugs, mice, rabbits or any small mammal that it can catch, carrion and chickens.

NATURAL FOOD FOR MAMMALS AND REPTILES

The trick here is to make sure that your garden is a good breeding ground for beetles, bugs, worms, slugs and all the other creatures that will in turn feed mammals and reptiles. You might not like the idea of giving a home to slugs, for example, but just think of all the slug-eating mammals and reptiles such as hedgehogs and badgers that will be attracted by your delicious slugs. (See pages 54–55 for planting suggestions.)

WHAT DO REPTILES EAT?

- *Coronella austriaca* **(Smooth Snake)** – Beetles, bugs, worms, small birds and small mammals.

- *Natrix natrix* **(Grass Snake) and** *Opheodrys vernalis* **(Green Grass Snake)** – Insects, frogs, slugs and small mammals.

- *Vipera berus* **(Adder)** – Insects, bugs, lizards, frogs, newts, birds and small mammals.

- *Zootoca vivipara* **(Common Lizard)** – Insects, beetles, spiders, bugs and plants.

Small mammals

Which small mammals are common in gardens?

The wonderful thing about small mammals is that you do not have to lure them in. If you lower your defences and hold back on your prejudices, they will come in uninvited. There is no need, either, to worry about the dangers of, for example, plague rats or vast populations of rabbits, because if you get the balance right in your garden the various wildlife groups will regulate each other.

Mus musculus

House Mouse

Size – 7.5–10 cm (3–4 in) from nose to tail.

Appearance – Grey-brown with lighter grey-brown tones on the underparts.

Habitat – Often seen in hedges and bushes in parks, allotments and gardens.

Food – Insects, larvae, berries, seeds and discarded human food – in fact, everything that is available.

Home – In houses, sheds, and just about anywhere where there is a dry hole.

Comments – You might not like mice, but there are plenty of wild animals that do. Keep them out of your house by cleaning up food and sealing up rubbish containers (block up any holes), and then make sure your garden invites in mice-eating animals such as hedgehogs, badgers, weasels, birds of prey and snakes. In case you are thinking of opening your home to house mice, just remember that a healthy female will give birth to 40–60 young in a good year!

Adult feeding young

Oryctolagus cuniculus

Rabbit

Size – 40–48 cm (16–19 in) long.

Appearance – Brown-grey-yellow with white undersides to the belly, chest, legs and tail.

Habitat – Farmland, heathland, commons, wasteland and gardens.

Food – Grasses, garden plants and crops.

Home – Lives underground in burrows and holes, sometimes in extensive burrow systems or warrens.

Comments – Breeds from late winter through to summer. Rabbits can be a bit of a pest, but their presence will attract birds of prey and larger mammals such as foxes. Rabbits can exhibit huge fluctuations in population – one day there may be hundreds, the next they contract myxomatosis (a viral disease) and their numbers are decimated.

Rabbits feeding near the burrow

Rattus norvegicus

Brown Rat

Size – 20–23 cm (8–9 in) long, not counting a tail half as long as the body.

Appearance – Grey-brown-red coat with white underparts.

Habitat – Farms, gardens, parks and houses.

Food – Roots, shoots, insects, farm and garden produce, and discarded human food – everything that is available.

Home – Anywhere where it can dig, burrow or hide, in holes, houses, sheds and barns.

Adult eating kitchen scraps

Comments – Breeds throughout the year but especially in spring and autumn. While rats are frequently blamed for spreading disease and despoiling food and crops, current research suggests that a healthy rat living in a wildlife garden is no worse than a squirrel. If you really do not like rats, then you must limit your food handouts – do not leave uncovered food either for you or your pets in and around the home. Make sure they cannot get into your home, garage, shed or cellar, and invite in creatures like owls and snakes that feed on rats. (Be aware that if you poison rats you will in effect also be killing the creatures that feed on them.)

Sciurus vulgaris

Grey Squirrel

Size – 23–30 cm (9–12 in) long, not including the tail which is 20–23 cm (8–9 in) long.

Appearance – Has a grey coat, with white underparts, and a hint of orange-brown on the back, tail and head.

Habitat – Woodland, parks and gardens.

Food – Bark, buds, shoots, seeds, nuts (especially hazelnuts), acorns, berries, fungi, insects and even birds' eggs and nestlings; will also take supplementary food put out for birds.

Home – Makes a nest or 'drey' in the crown of a tree.

Comments – Grey squirrels are very common, and extremely agile. If you do not want them to eat your bird food, there are many 'squirrel-proof' feeders on the market. They are very ingenious when it comes to food, but that is part of their charm.

Adult eating an acorn

Talpa europaea

Mole

Size – 13–20 cm (5–8 in) long.

Appearance – Has a barrel-shaped body with velvety, silvery grey-brown-black hair, paddle-shaped legs and a long, pink-ended snout.

Habitat – Gardens, parks and woodland.

Adult

Food – Worms, slugs, insects and larvae.

Home – Elaborate, many-chambered burrows.

Comments – If you are a lawn-lover, then you probably do not like moles. The truth is that, while they do make a mess, they are incredibly beautiful and well-adapted creatures. If you are lucky enough to have moles, focus on the wonderful way that they loosen and aerate the soil, and eat all manner of small creatures.

Moles love eating worms

Hedgehogs and badgers

Do these animals pose any risks?

The hedgehog is a shy, harmless creature that uses its prickles as a defence mechanism, rolling up into a ball when danger looms. The spines are sharp, so you should avoid handling them. Badgers are beautiful animals but they have been associated with spreading the cattle disease bovine tuberculosis or TB, they can be aggressive, and they need a lot of space. If you already have badgers in your garden, leave them alone and enjoy them from a distance.

Erinaceus europaea

Hedgehog

Size – 25–30 cm (10–12 in) long.

Appearance – Grey-brown with white-brown undersides; back covered in spines.

Habitat – Farmland, the bottom of hedges, woodland, wasteland and gardens.

Food – Slugs, worms, snails, frogs, mice – just about anything that is small and slow enough to be caught.

Home – Holes and little dry places under hedges and buildings.

Comments – The name comes from the Old English 'hegge hoge', meaning 'hedge pig'. In times of stress, a hedgehog is able to roll into a tight ball, so that the spines all point outwards. The main predators or dangers are humans (especially their cars), dogs, ferrets, rats, weasels, owls and hawks. Hedgehogs are mainly nocturnal, but they can sometimes be seen during the day. They will hibernate if conditions are right. If you really want to get rid of garden pests such as slugs, snails, aphids and insects, hedgehogs are the answer. They are very susceptible to insecticides, however, so if you use these you will in effect be killing hedgehogs.

Adult

HEDGEHOG PROTECTION

Hedgehogs are vulnerable creatures and it pays to take steps to ensure their safety in your garden.

- When burning a pile of leaves, always check that the pile is not giving a home to a hedgehog.
- Do not use slug pellets; first they kill the slugs and then the hedgehogs that feed on the slugs.
- Swimming pools can be death traps; hedgehogs fall in and cannot get out.
- Fine plastic netting can be a problem; hedgehogs become entangled and then starve.
- Take care when using a lawnmower or strimmer, as hedgehogs can easily be killed by these machines.

Hedgehogs eat many of the creatures we consider to be pests, such as slugs.

Meles meles

Badger

Size – 82–90 cm (32–36 in) long. A healthy adult weighs in at 9–14 kg (20–30 lb), depending on the time of year.

Appearance – Grey-black and white, with distinctive black and white markings on the face.

Habitat – Farmland, heathland, woodland, common land, wasteland and large gardens.

Food – Roots, shoots, fruits, insects, worms, small animals; will also eat kitchen scraps.

Home – Lives in a maze of underground holes, tunnels and chambers called a sett. Research suggests that setts are passed down from one generation to the next.

Comments – Badgers live in family groups of 10–15 adults, and are known to live up to 15 years. Research suggests that there are at least 250,000 badgers in the UK. Badgers are rarely seen in daytime. The problem with TB, badgers and cattle is complicated and confused, with various for-and-against groups coming up with contradictory views. Just be aware that not everyone is a badger-lover.

WARNING: An injured or cornered badger is dangerous and could easily injure children or pets. If you have badgers, do not intervene – just observe them from a distance.

Adult drinking

It is very unusual to see a badger in daylight. They normally start to emerge from the sett after dusk and are active through the night.

Lizards and snakes

To attract lizards and snakes to your garden, all you can do is ensure that the conditions are right. You need a good-sized pond (see pages 18–21) to give a home to the creatures that snakes like to eat – frogs, fish, toads and newts – as well as areas of stones and sand for lizards. In an area where both snakes and lizards are found, the likelihood is that snakes will be more numerous because they will feed on the lizards.

Natrix natrix

Grass Snake

Size – 0.9–1.2 m (3–4 ft) long.

Appearance – Usually green-grey-olive colour, with black bars running down the sides, and a yellow-white or orange patch around the neck. Black variations also occur.

Habitat – Farmland, heathland, woodland, common land, wasteland and large gardens.

Food – Frogs, toads, fish, newts, lizards and small mammals.

Home – Lives in holes, under logs and rocks, in hedge bottoms – anywhere that is warm, dry and sheltered.

Comments – The female is larger than the male. The white marking around the neck is the reason why in some areas it was traditionally called the 'common ringed snake'. Grass Snakes hibernate over winter, emerge and mate in spring, and lay eggs in summer. Although when threatened the grass snake sometimes strikes an attacking pose, and may even bite if provoked, it is completely harmless to humans. *Opheodrys vernalis* (Green Grass Snake, Smooth Green Snake) is a similar species that is native to North America.

Grass snakes will eat frogs

FEAR OF SNAKES

Research suggests that if you show the average person in the street a slideshow of creepy and dangerous plants and animals – mushrooms, slimy plants, rats, spiders, frogs, snakes and so on – invariably they will show greater fear when they see the snakes. Research also suggests that evolution has programmed mammals to fear poisonous animals, especially snakes. Some snakes, such as adders (see page 64), are poisonous and should be treated with extreme caution. The truth is, however, that snakes are more scared of us than we are of them and will only bite or attack if provoked, so if you treat the snake with respect it should do the same for you.

A pair of grass snakes basking in the early morning sun.

Zootoca vivipara

Common Lizard

Size – 15–18 cm (6–7 in) long.

Appearance – Dark black-brown with short legs and a yellow-orange underbelly. The male has more brightly coloured underparts, ranging from orange-yellow to red. The female's underparts are paler, more white-to-yellow than orange.

Habitat – Sunny, dry, rocky to sandy common land and heathland.

Food – Insects, spiders, bugs and other small creatures.

Home – Holes and dry places under hedges, rocks, logs and buildings.

Comments – The common lizard has learnt to adapt to its environment – for example, in mountainous regions it lives in damp areas, while in more lowland regions it prefers open, dry conditions. If the lizard is under attack, it can shed its tail to escape, and grow a new one. This species is the only one in its genus that is 'viviparous', meaning it produces live young rather than eggs.

Basking in the sun

A stone wall is perfect for basking lizards

WHAT DO LIZARDS EAT?

- *Cnemidophorus gularis* **(Texas Spotted Whiptail; Southern States of the USA)** – small insects and other lizards.

- *Elgaria multicarinata* **(Southern Alligator Lizard; coast of North America and Southern California)** – most small insects, flies, spiders and crickets.

- *Lacerta agilis* **(Sand Lizard; Europe and Asia)** – flies, beetles, locusts and spiders.

- *Ophisaurus attenuatus* **(Slender Glass Lizard; USA)** – flies, spiders and just about anything else it can find.

- *Podarcis muralis* **(Wall Lizard; Europe and Mediterranean islands)** – most small insects.

- *Podarcis taurica* **(Balkan Wall Lizard; Asia and Europe)** – insects, spiders, bugs and almost any small creature it can catch.

Common lizards can be spotted sunning themselves on a rock or stone wall.

Other wild animals

The wonderful thing about wildlife gardens is that you can never know what is going to pop up next. For example, in the past our garden has been visited by a family of wild boar. If you are lucky, you might catch sight of a deer, an adder or a slow worm or, if your garden backs on to a river, stream or canal, even a mink, a stoat or a water vole. If you are quiet and still – no cracking twigs or leaves underfoot – and just watch, there are many exciting possibilities.

Will anything unusual visit my garden?

UNUSUAL SPECIES YOU MIGHT SEE

Sus scrofa (Wild Boar)

Size – 1.4–1.5 m (4¾–5 ft) long.

Appearance – Compact with a large head and dense, bristly fur.

Habitat – Woodland, common land and scrubland.

Food – Grass, roots, shoots, foliage and worms.

Comments – The wild boar is an omnivorous mammal found across Europe, Asia and the UK.

Dama dama (Fallow Deer)

Size – 89–96 cm (35–38 in) from ground to shoulder.

Appearance – Reddish orange-brown with white spots on the back and flanks, and cream-white underparts. The male grows broad-bladed antlers annually.

Food – Grass, brambles, foliage.

Habitat – Woodland, parks and open spaces, large country gardens and wooded riverbanks.

Viperus berus (Adder)

Size – 60–96 cm (24–38 in) long.

Appearance – Grey-brown, with grey-white zigzag and dot patterns along the body, and a 'V' mark on the back of the head.

Food – Small animals such as mice, voles, lizards and frogs.

Habitat – Woodland, fields, hedgerows, scrubby sand dunes, farmland and country gardens.

Comments – The poisonous bite is painful and can make you very ill, but rarely deadly. Seek prompt medical attention if bitten.

Anguis fragilis (Slow Worm)

Size – 25–50 cm (10–20 in) long.

Appearance – Shiny silver-grey to silver-gold.

Habitat – Common land, sandy scrubland, stony wasteland, and dry, warm, sheltered gardens.

Food – Insects, worms and slugs.

Comments – The slow worm is a legless lizard, not a snake.

UNUSUAL SPECIES YOU MIGHT SEE (CONTINUED)

Neomys fodiens (Water Shrew)

Size – 7.5–13 cm (3–5 in) long.

Appearance – Black-brown with silver-grey-white underparts.

Food – Worms, slugs, insects and small fish.

Habitat – Rivers, streams, ponds, marshes and damp farmland and gardens.

Mustela nivalis (Weasel)

Size – 25–30 cm (10–12 in) from nose to tail.

Appearance – Reddish nut-brown with creamy brown-white underparts.

Food – Rats, mice, voles – anything it can catch.

Habitat – Woodland, fields, open spaces near towns, and large gardens.

Mustela erminea (Stoat)

Size – 25–35 cm (10–14 in) from nose to tail.

Appearance – Reddish brown with creamy brown-white underparts, and a black tip to the end of the tail.

Food – Rats, mice, voles, rabbits; anything it can catch.

Habitat – Woodland, farmland, fields, rocky scrubland, open spaces in towns, large wild gardens.

Rattus rattus (Black Rat)

Size – 18–23 cm (7–9 in) long plus an 18–23 cm (7–9 in) tail.

Appearance – Black-brown with large, pink ears and a tail that is at least as long as the body.

Food – Most crops but prefers grain.

Habitat – Gardens, buildings and structures near coastal areas.

Lampetra planeri (Brook Lamprey)

Size – 38–60 cm (15–24 in) long.

Appearance – Silver-grey-brown with gill holes along the side of the body, and distinctive, primitive, jawless sucker-mouth.

Food – Fine particles in water.

Habitat – Brooks, streams.

Arvicola terrestris (Water Vole)

Size – 20–30 cm (8–12 in) long from nose to tail, about one-third of the total length being the tail.

Appearance – Dark black-brown with a round, short-nosed face and fur-covered ears.

Food – Riverside plants.

Habitat – Lives in and around slow-flowing water, such as ponds, streams, rivers and canals.

Mustela vison (American Mink)

Size – 45–60 cm (18–24 in) from nose to tail.

Appearance – Reddish brown through to pinky-cream and black-brown.

Food – Fish, birds – almost anything it can catch.

Habitat – Streams, rivers, lakes, ponds, wet woodland and gardens that border rivers and canals.

Comments – There are now large wild populations of this mink, descended from ancestors that escaped from fur farms throughout Europe, in many places driving out its cousin *Mustela lutreola* (European Mink).

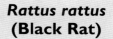

About insects and other small creatures

Why are small creatures so vital?

Each insect and small creature is important in its own right – every ant, aphid and earwig is a miracle of nature. Furthermore, these sometimes not-so-endearing creatures are the very stuff that keeps the great wheel turning by slotting into the food chain. If we could eliminate our particular insect and bug hates, then all the creatures that feed on them, and those higher up the chain, would ultimately starve (see page 57).

INSECTS AND SMALL CREATURES IN THE GARDEN

One good look at your garden will show you that the greater part of the permanent wildlife population is made up of insects and other small creatures. There will be seasonal visitors, such as birds, bats, mice, squirrels and rabbits (and some of these might stay over), and one or two dynamic creatures such as badgers, foxes and grass snakes may come in to hunt the visitors; but at the heart of every wildlife garden there will be a fixed population of thousands of creeping and crawling, wriggling and squiggling, buzzing and humming, flitting and stinging creatures. If you need proof of this, go out on a warm summer evening and lift the lid on your compost heap, or have a close-up look at the mud in the pond, and you will see that the compost or mud is teeming with life. It is the same in every corner of the garden – there is life under every leaf, rock and stone.

WHAT DO THEY EAT?

In very general terms, these creatures feed on pollen, nectar, vegetable matter, smaller creatures in the soil, and each other. Gardeners all know about caterpillars feasting on cabbages, and aphids on roses, but as for what feeds on the caterpillars and the aphids, most people never get to know because they are so busy rushing about with chemical sprays. The interesting thing is that, if you hold the chemical spraying back long enough, you will see ants coming in for the aphids and birds coming in for just about everything. So the best way of feeding your small creatures is simply to get on with your gardening and let nature do the rest. Certainly, some of your plants will suffer in the short term, but it will all work out when a balance is achieved.

CHILDREN AND SMALL CREATURES

Children love watching insects and small creatures. If you want to interest them in how everything interacts with everything else in the natural world, sit them down in a quiet corner of the garden and show them an ants' nest, or perhaps ladybirds feeding on aphids. Once they appreciate that every stone, leaf and twig gives shelter to creatures, they will have some understanding of what makes wildlife tick. Children enjoy lists, facts and figures – how many worms there are in a certain area of ground, the longest snake, the number of different bugs in a garden, the size and weight of an owl pellet. Most enjoy collecting, and like things that are a bit creepy or smelly. Set them tasks like making a collection of different bugs, mice skulls or snake skins. If taking a group of children on a field trip, however, remember that some kids really dislike such things.

POINTS TO CONSIDER

- More compost heaps, and more tree, leaf and plant debris, equate with more insects and small creatures.

- A muddy-bottomed wildlife pond is always a good option because it makes a wonderful home for bugs.

- Trying to achieve a good balance is something to aim for – it is not going to happen overnight.

- Balance is achieved by making sure that each creature has natural enemies to keep it in check – ants to eat aphids, various flies and bugs to eat the aphids, birds to eat the flies, and so on. An imbalance will occur when one of the links in the chain is broken.

- Ladybirds multiply in summer and are voracious eaters of aphids, mites and thrips.

- Aphids excrete honeydew, which attracts ants, which attract birds.

- Woodlice eat organic material such as leaves and dead wood, and birds and mice eat woodlice.

- Whitefly attract birds.

- Beetles make a tasty feed for many small birds.

- Spiders eat flies and small insects, and creatures such as mice, lizards and birds eat spiders.

COMMON EXAMPLES

Redcurrants are eaten by aphids, which in turn are eaten by birds.

The insects on this plant — a mixture of flies, beetles and blackfly — will make a tasty meal for a family of blue tits.

A spider wrapping up its prey in a web cocoon for storage.

Woodlice (see page 77) cleaning up rotten wood debris.

These aphids, if left untreated with pesticides, make a tasty meal for ladybirds. Ants, however, will 'farm' aphids — to feed on their honeydew — and protect them from predators.

Planning and planting the garden

Do I really want to encourage them?

The wonderful thing about insects and creepy-crawlies is that you do not have to do much to keep them happy, other than leave them alone. If you stop splashing chemicals around, they will do very nicely. However, if you build a pond (see pages 18–21), and a handful of compost heaps, and are more selective with your planting, then you will most certainly be able to increase the range of small creatures in your garden.

DESIGN CONSIDERATIONS

- **Wild areas** – Allow some part of the garden to become overgrown and wild. Plant a wildflower meadow, and set one or two corners aside for weeds. Reduce the mown lawn to a minimum.
- **Food** – Have dense borders with lots of shrubs and ground-cover plants, with as many berry-bearing species as possible. Allow the grass to grow long, and back the whole picture with as many trees as the space allows. Double up on the number of vegetables that you plant – so that you allow half for you and half for the insects.
- **Water** – Go for the biggest possible pond, with related bog gardens and pools. Have water butts to collect rain water.
- **Shelter** – Stack up piles of logs, build stone cairns and walls, collect piles of leaves and build boxes for insects.

If you plant in swathes, so that one clump of flowers runs into another and the ground is well covered, you will provide a home for beneficial insects and small creatures.

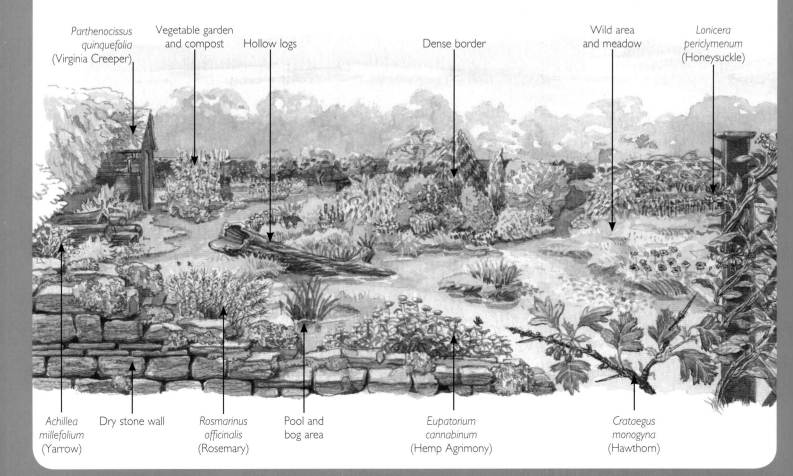

Parthenocissus quinquefolia (Virginia Creeper)

Vegetable garden and compost

Hollow logs

Dense border

Wild area and meadow

Lonicera periclymenum (Honeysuckle)

Achillea millefolium (Yarrow)

Dry stone wall

Rosmarinus officinalis (Rosemary)

Pool and bog area

Eupatorium cannabinum (Hemp Agrimony)

Crataegus monogyna (Hawthorn)

WHERE TO START

To create an environment that encourages diversity, a good first step is to build compost heaps. The compost will encourage micro-organisms to flourish – these will feed creatures such as bugs and ants, which will provide food for birds, reptiles and mammals. The next step is to encourage plant-pollinating creatures such as butterflies and bees.

PLANTS FOR BUTTERFLIES

- *Aster aestivus* (**Michaelmas Daisy**) – Hardy, with dense heads of white, star-shaped flowers.

- *Buddleja officinalis* (**Buddleia**) – Grows well against sunny walls; the purple flowers attract butterflies and other insects.

- *Erica erigena* (**Irish heath**) – Hardy, with mauve-pink flowers.

- *Eupatorium cannabinum* – (**Hemp agrimony**) – Grows wild and likes damp places.

- *Knautia arvensis* (**Field Scabious**) – Hardy, with lots of pincushion-like, bluish lilac flowers.

- *Origanum vulgare* (**Marjoram**) – Grows wild, hardy, with dark green leaves and mauve flowers.

- *Syringa vulgaris* (**Lilac**) – Shrub or small tree with very fragrant, pink, lilac or bluish flowers.

- *Urtica dioica* (**Stinging Nettle**) – Grows wild, with serrated leaves that sting on contact with skin. An important food plant for caterpillars.

PLANTS FOR BEES

- *Daucus carota* (**Carrot**) – Familiar vegetable that always seems to attract bees.

- *Lonicera periclymenum* (**Honeysuckle**) – Hardy, grows wild, and attracts bees, butterflies and other insects.

- *Parthenocissus quinquefolia* (**Virginia Creeper**) – Hardy, a good screen plant, grows wild.

- *Rosmarinus officinalis* (**Rosemary**) – Hardy herb that has a delicious fragrance when the leaves are crushed.

- *Rubus fruticosus* (**Blackberry or Bramble**) – Hardy, grows wild and attracts a broad range of insects.

- *Trifolium* **spp.** (**Clover**) – Hardy, with types to suit all situations.

- *Vicia faba* (**Broad Bean**) – Hardy vegetable that bears pea-like flowers.

The plant coverage and the different heights here will give home to a good variety of butterflies, bees and insects.

PLANTS FOR OTHER INSECTS

- *Achillea millefolium* (Yarrow) – Hardy, with clusters of daisy-like flowers.

- *Centaurea cyanus* (Cornflower) – Hardy, with blue, thistle-like flowers.

- *Crataegus monogyna* (Hawthorn) – Hardy, grows wild and makes a good wildlife hedge.

- *Eschscholzia californica* (Californian Poppy) – Hardy, with brightly coloured, saucer-shaped flowers.

- *Foeniculum vulgare* (Fennel) – Hardy, with fern-like, aromatic leaves and clusters of small yellow flowers.

A peacock butterfly (see page 70) feeding on a yellow variety of buddleia (see above).

Butterflies and moths

What is the difference?

There can be no finer sight than a garden full of flowers at the height of summer festooned with beautiful butterflies of various sizes and colours. Butterflies and moths are winged insects that have a number of common characteristics as well as some significant differences (see below). Butterflies will only fly when the temperature is high enough, and will sometimes lay their wings flat in a sunny spot in order to warm them up.

MAIN DIFFERENCES

Butterflies and moths belong to the same insect family (Lepidoptera), and at first sight look much alike, but there are four clear differences:
- Butterflies gather food during the day and moths do this during the night.
- Butterflies make shiny chrysalises and moths make silky cocoons.
- Butterflies usually rest with their wings closed and moths with their wings open.
- Butterflies have long, thin antennae and moths have short, feathery ones.

BREEDING CYCLE

The adults mate and lay eggs, which hatch into caterpillars. After a period of voracious feeding (as most gardeners will tell you!), each caterpillar turns into a 'pupa', which is housed either in a chrysalis (butterflies) or a cocoon (moths), and becomes dormant. When conditions are right, the adult emerges and the cycle begins all over again.

COMMON BUTTERFLIES

***Aglais urticae* (Small Tortoiseshell)** – Wingspan 5 cm (2 in); brightly coloured with speckled orange and black wings; caterpillar black and yellow; feeds on many plants including thistles, nettles and buddleia.

***Pieris brassicae* (Large White, European Large White)** – Wingspan 6 cm (2½ in); white with black dots; caterpillar mottled green and black; feeds on most members of the cabbage family.

***Pyronia tithonus* (Gatekeeper)** – Wingspan 3.5 cm (1½ in); bright orange-brown with brown wing edges and dotted 'eye'; caterpillar brown with white stripes; feeds on many nectar-rich flowers and plants in and around gardens, orchards and hedgerows.

***Inachis io* (Peacock)** – Wingspan 6 cm (2½ in); bright red, black and blue, with peacock 'eye'; caterpillar black and hairy; feeds on garden flowers, buddleia and rotting fruit.

***Polyommatus icarus* (Common Blue)** – Wingspan 3.5 cm (1½ in); brightly coloured blue and blue-black with red-orange wing-edge lines and dots; caterpillar green; feeds on many plants including clover and fleabane.

***Vanessa atalanta* (Red Admiral, American Red Admiral)** – Wingspan 6 cm (2½ in); black with bold red and white markings; caterpillar green and yellow; feeds on many plants including Michaelmas daisy, buddleia and clover.

COMMON MOTHS

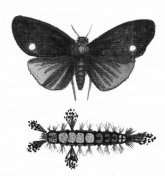

***Abraxas grossulariata* (Magpie Moth)** – Wingspan 4 cm (1¾ in); black and white/cream wings, with red, orange and black details; looper caterpillar same colour as the adult's wings; feeds on many plants including gooseberry bushes, fruit trees and hazel.

***Erannis defoliaria* (Mottled Umber)** – Wingspan 3.5 cm (1½ in); mottled brown-cream-white wings; caterpillar fat and brown; feeds on the leaves and buds of fruit trees.

***Orgyia antiqua* (Vapourer Moth)** – Wingspan 38 mm (1⅜ in); red-brown with dark-coloured wing 'eye'; caterpillar yellow, red and green with exotic tufts of hair; feeds on a range of garden trees and shrubs.

***Choreutis pariana* (Apple Leaf Skeletonizer)** – Wingspan 12 mm (½ in); small with peachy red and brown striped wings; caterpillar fat, yellow and green with black dots; feeds on crab apple and other fruit trees; gets its name because of the way it skeletonizes the leaves.

***Hepialus lupulinus* (Common Swift, European Common Swift)** – Wingspan 3.5 cm (1½ in); mottled brown with darker details; caterpillar yellow/brown, resembles a maggot; feeds on crops such as wheat and lettuce.

***Plutella xylostella* (Diamond-back Moth)** – Wingspan 12 mm (½ in); small and fly-shaped with brown and white, feather-edged wings; caterpillar plump and green; feeds on a broad range of plants, including many common vegetables.

***Elophila nymphaeata* (Brown China-mark)** – Wingspan 3 cm (1¼ in); dull, mottled, creamy brown; caterpillar cream and brown, resembles a maggot; feeds on many water plants in and around ponds.

***Hydraecia micacea* (Rosy Rustic)** – Wingspan 3.5 cm (1½ in); light to dark brown shaded wings; caterpillar pinky red, yellow and brown; feeds on grasses and crops such as tomatoes and potatoes.

***Spilosoma lubricipeda* (White Ermine)** – Wingspan 4 cm (1¾ in); furry white with black spots; caterpillar green/brown with dark details; feeds on leaves, including oak.

Bees and wasps

What is the difference between them?

Wasps and bees are closely related, and both are insects that build colonies around a central queen. The visible difference is that wasps are bald and bees are hairy. The less obvious difference is that wasps feed their meat-eating larvae dead insects, while bees feed their vegetarian larvae pollen and nectar. Although they are both capable of inflicting a nasty sting when provoked, they have a very useful role to play in the garden.

A honey bee extracting nectar from a flower.

POINTS TO CONSIDER

- Research suggests that bees are one of our favourite insects and that bee-keeping is a very popular gardening activity.
- The worker honey bee has a life span of about four weeks, but the honey bee queen has a life span of about five years.
- Bees feed on nectar and pollen, and are used as pollinators by many flowering plants.
- Honey bees need to eat about 9 kg (20 lb) of honey for each 450 g (1 lb) of beeswax.
- Wasps feed their larvae on insects and spiders, and the adults eat nectar and other sweet substances.
- Although unprovoked attacks by wasps are rare, the fact is that people do get stung and do have allergic reactions. Wasps are particularly attracted by sweet, sticky foods and drinks, so avoid consuming these in the open air in summer if you do not want to attract them.

Apis mellifera

Honey Bee

Size – Queen 2.5 cm (1 in), worker 15 mm (⅝ in), drone 18 mm (¾ in) long.

Appearance – Has brown and yellow, fuzzy body.

Comments – Lives in a colony, usually in a beehive. The queen lays eggs, workers collect nectar and pollen, build cells and tend larvae, and drones or males have no purpose other than to mate with the queen. They forage within a 3 km (2 mile) radius of the hive. Honey bees use nectar to make honey – a complex mix of water and sugars. The bees get nectar from flowers, return to the hive, pass the nectar to other worker bees, spread the nectar throughout the honeycombs, and so on until it becomes the thick syrup that we know as honey.

Drone

Worker

Queen

Bombus terrestris

Bumble Bee

Size – 15 mm (⅝ in) long.

Appearance – Short and plump, with black and yellow bands around the body, and a white tail.

Comments – Nests underground in holes in a sheltered position. Only fertilized queens live through winter. The colony is not permanent and dies out in autumn.

Female

Underground nest

Vespa crabro

Hornet (UK) European Hornet (USA)

Size – 3 cm (1¼ in) long.

Appearance – Has very bright orange and brown markings.

Comments – Nests in dead or dying trees and rotting wood. The adults feed the larvae with dead insects, and in return the larvae provide the adults with sweet saliva. They use the saliva mixed with chewed wood to make the nest.

Female

Vespula vulgaris

Common Wasp (UK) Yellowjacket Wasp (USA)

Size – 2.5 cm (1 in) long.

Appearance – Has distinct black and yellow stripes.

Wasps love ripe fruit

Comments – Nests in a hole in a bank, wall, house roof, or anywhere where it is warm and sheltered. The nest consists of 'papery' cells made from chewed wood and saliva. Once the egg-laying season is over, the adults feed on ripe fruit.

Worker

A wasps' nest is made, initially by a queen, from a mixture of chewed-up wood and saliva. It is later extended by workers.

Slugs and snails

Gardeners often get hot under the collar when their food crops are decimated by slugs and snails, but the fact is that every creature has a place in the natural scheme of things. You may not care much for slugs and snails, but research suggests that creatures such as lizards, slow worms, grass snakes, hedgehogs, ground beetles, toads, some frogs, thrushes and crows regard them as a tasty morsel, so refrain from using pellets.

Slugs

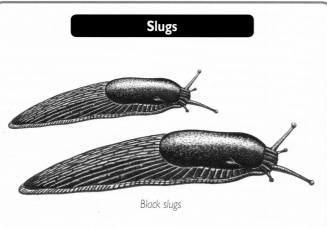

Black slugs

Arion ater
Black Slug (UK) European Black Slug (USA)

Size – 13–18 cm (5–7 in) long.

Appearance – Colours vary from black through to red, white and orange; has a distinctive saddle shape with a nostril hole to one side.

Comments – Eats garden crops but prefers rotting vegetation, manure and compost heap materials. The more compost heaps you have, the less chance that the slugs will attack your crops.

Field slug

Deroceras reticulatum
Field Slug

Size – 2.5–5 cm (1–2 in) long.

Appearance – Grey-fawn in colour with black-brown fleck markings; has a ridge along the back.

Comments – Lives in damp farmland and gardens, and eats everything from lettuce to potatoes.

Two slugs mating – the white blob is their genitalia. Note the off-centre nostril hole at the side of the head saddle.

A well-fed, healthy snail can live for up to three years – note the skirt- or sucker-like feet that grip close to the ground.

Snails

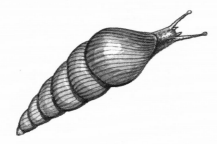

Balea perversa
Tree Snail

Size – 9 mm (⅜ in) long.

Appearance – Very small, with a long, narrow, cornucopia-shaped shell.

Comments – Lives under the bark of trees. Tree snails come in many colours, depending upon their food and habitat.

Helix aspersa
Garden Snail

Size – 3.5 cm (1½ in) long.

Appearance – Has a wrinkled shell with brown, fawn and cream markings.

Comments – Lives for 2–3 years, and is eaten by many wild birds; very common in enclosed gardens. The colour and the number of bands relates to the food, habitat and age of the snail.

Cepaea hortensis
White-lipped Snail

Size – 15 mm (⅝ in) long.

Appearance – Has a bright white-yellow shell with darker yellow-brown markings.

Comments – Lives in a range of habitats, including woods and hedges. In small, enclosed, high-walled gardens, the colour of the snail's shell will reflect the colour of the walls.

Helix pomatia
Roman Snail

Size – 3 cm (1¼ in) long.

Appearance – Has a wrinkled shell with creamy markings.

Comments – Favoured by Romans as a delicacy, hence the common name; lives in chalky areas and is now a rare and protected species.

POINTS TO CONSIDER

- If you kill slugs with chemicals, you will indirectly kill wildlife higher up the food chain. Research confirms that slug pellets kill creatures such as hedgehogs and birds.
- You could search around for reports that list known slug-eating creatures, and you could positively encourage these creatures onto your patch. For example, you could build log piles to give home to creatures like hedgehogs.
- Research suggests that the tree snail travels the world by sticking to the underside of the wings of migratory birds.
- Many common snail species are edible. If you are going to eat your snails, make sure they have not come into contact with any chemicals. To do this, catch them and feed them for a week or so, until any toxins have gone through their systems.

- Although snails are hermaphrodite – meaning they are both male and female – they still need to mate with another snail.
- The very fact that snail breeders have to proactively protect their snails against mice, shrews and birds suggests that garden snails do have predators and will attract wildlife.
- If you do have a lot of snails on your plot, to the extent that you think that you need to eat them before they eat your garden, you need to make sure that they are not protected.
- Observation and folklore indicate that some birds have learnt to break open the shells not only by beating them on stones but also by dropping them from a good height.
- The best way to eat snails is to fry them with butter and lots of garlic, and serve with home-made brown bread.

Beetles, bugs and creepy-crawlies

Must I learn to love them?

It is not easy to love creatures that variously scavenge, eat dead organic matter, sting, suck fluids through syringe-like mouthparts, give off strange smells, and generally slurp and munch their way right through your garden. Instead, try to see them as a means to an end, so that, when you are faced with 'pests' such as aphids, you simply identify their natural enemies and proactively invite them in for a feast. Here are some common beetles, bugs and creepy-crawlies.

Agriotes lineatus (Click Beetle)

12 mm (½ in) long; larvae are known as 'wireworms' and adults sometimes as 'flip' beetles; eats garden plants; larvae are eaten by hedgehogs, mice and bugs.

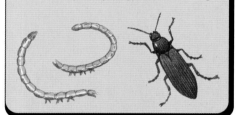

Anthonomus pomorum (Apple Blossom Weevil)

6 mm (¼ in) long; feeds on buds in early spring. Natural enemies include parasitic wasps.

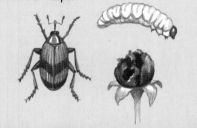

Blennocampa phyllocolpa (Rose Sawfly)

18 mm (¾ in) long; larvae feed on leaves and are important food for a range of birds, small mammals and insects.

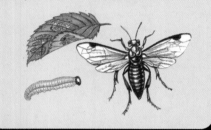

Chorthippus brunneus (Grasshopper)

18 mm (¾ in) long; feeds on grasses and various plants; important food for birds, toads, snakes and mammals.

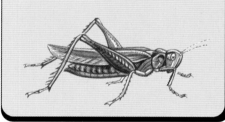

Chrysopa carnea (Lacewing)

3 cm (1¼ in) long; feeds on nectar, aphids and some soft-bodied larvae; is itself food for birds, mammals and bugs.

Cicadella viridis (Green Leafhopper)

6 mm (¼ in) long; jumps from plant to plant; thousands of types; eats sap from grasses and similar plants; important food for birds, lizards, spiders and bugs.

Adalia bipunctata (Two-spot Ladybird)

6 mm (¼ in) long; eats other creatures, including aphids; important food for beetles, bugs and some birds.

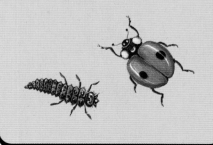

Contarinia pyrivora (Pear Midge)

3 mm (⅛ in) long; larvae eat the fruit of the pear tree; important food for all manner of other insects and birds.

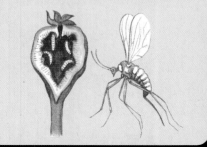

Crioceris asparagi (Asparagus Beetle)

12 mm (½ in) long; feeds on foliage; larvae are food for birds and mice.

Delia radicum (Cabbage Root Fly)

9 mm (⅜ in) long; larvae feed on roots and are an important food for beetles.

Lasius niger (Black Ant)

3 mm (⅛ in); eats aphids; food for birds, lizards, snakes, frogs and toads.

Lygocoris pabulinus (Green Capsid Bug)

6 mm (¼ in) long; eats plant juices; eaten by mites and nematodes.

Macrosiphum rosae (Rose Aphid)

3 mm (⅛ in); eats farm and garden plants; important food for ladybirds, ants, other insects and lacewings.

Melolontha melolontha (Cockchafer)

2.5 cm (1 in) long; nocturnal beetle, sometimes called a 'maybug'; eats crops and trees; important food for bats, mice, lizards, snakes and birds.

Merodon equestris (Narcissus Bulb Fly)

12 mm (½ in) long; looks like a small bee; larvae eat bulbs and roots and are eaten by birds, small mammals and flies.

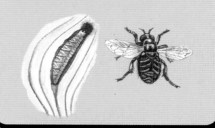

Oniscus asellus (Woodlouse)

12 mm (½ in) long; eats dead and dying wood and plant matter; food for hedge-hogs, lizards, owls, foxes, toads, frogs.

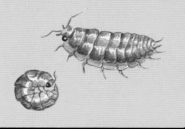

Phyllotreta spp. (Flea Beetles)

1.5 mm (¹⁄₁₆ in) long; eats farm and garden plants; natural predators include parasitic nematodes.

Syrphus ribesii (Hoverfly)

12 mm (½ in) long; eats vast numbers of aphids; important food for birds, small mammals and insects.

Blaniulus guttulatus (Spotted Snake Millipede)

3 cm (1¼ in) long; feeds on dead leaves and roots; food for small mammals such as moles and mice.

Tipula paludosa (Cranefly)

18 mm (¾ in) long; also known as 'daddylonglegs'; larvae or 'leatherjackets' eat plant roots; important food for lizards, toads and birds.

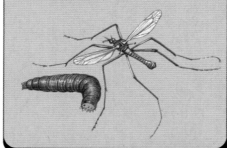

Forficula auricularia (Common Earwig)

9–15 mm (⅜–⅝ in) long; the name comes from the folklore that earwigs sometimes burrow down into the ears of humans to lay their eggs; they eat insects and plants such as clover, lettuce and plums.

Worms

Is there more than one type of worm?

Research suggests that there are at least a million different kinds of worm. They can be found in fresh water, in sea water, as parasites in plants and animals, in the food we eat, in our own bodies, and of course in the earth. In a garden, the two most common types are earthworms, which live in and condition the open soil, and composting worms, which can be brought in specially to speed up the composting process.

Eisenia foetida

Brandling, Red Wiggler, Tiger Worm

Size – 15 cm (6 in) long.

Comments – Lives on or near the surface of the compost in a wormery; does not tunnel into the ground; eats its own weight in moist organic matter every 24 hours.

Research suggests that the average country garden of 0.1 hectares (¼ acre) might contain anything up to a million worms.

Lumbricus terrestris

Common Earthworm

Size – 10–30 cm (4–12 in) long.

Comments – Takes plant matter down into the soil to eat. Research suggests that earthworm numbers are a measure of the world's well-being, with lots of earthworms equating with a healthy planet.

WORM COMPOSTING

This is a method of recycling organic waste and turning it into a valuable planting material, and it is usually faster than just leaving compost to its own devices. You need to buy a 'wormery', which is a special type of compost container, and must use suitable composting worms (not earthworms from your garden), commonly known as tiger worms, among other names (see above left). The number of worms you will need (they can be obtained by mail order), depend on the size of the wormery that you have bought; the producers generally recommend about 4,000 worms for a large set-up.

The worms will eat most organic kitchen waste – teabags, fruit, bread and cereals, for example. However, you must not give them garlic, potato peelings, food that has been treated with chemicals, or vinegar. The worms are hermaphrodite, and will breed freely within the wormery. If fed on a regular basis, the wormery will thrive and produce excellent garden compost.

Glossary

Algae Microscopic plants, mostly aquatic; in general terms, the green slime that forms on stagnant water.

Amphibious Describes creatures that live both on land and in water, such as frogs and newts.

Annual Plant that lives out its life – flowering, setting seed and dying – in a single growing season.

Aquatic plant Plant that can grow either in water or with its roots in saturated ground.

Biennial Plant that flowers and dies in its second growing season.

Biodiversity Number of plants or animals in a given area; a healthy environment has a diverse range of plants and animals.

Bog garden Area, usually close to a pond, where the soil is permanently wet or damp.

Bog plant Plant that will grow with its roots in wet or damp soil. Because some plants will grow in anything from moist ground through to shallow water, there is sometimes confusion between bog plants that enjoy very wet ground and emergent or marginal plants that enjoy growing in the outer margins of a pond.

Brackish Describes slightly salty, muddy water.

Clay soil Soil that has fine particles, making it sticky and poorly drained, but good for a pond.

Compost Well-rotted organic matter such as garden plant waste.

Deadheading Removal of a dead flower to encourage a plant to produce new growth and more flowers; this is a bad idea if you want to encourage seed production.

Deciduous Describes plants that shed their leaves at the end of the growing season.

Detritus Organic matter (derived from plants and animals); for example, all the dead leaves and insects under a bush or at the bottom of a pond.

Eco-friendly Not harmful or threatening to the environment.

Ecology Study of the relationships between living organisms and their environment; how animals, plants and humans are affected by and/or interact with the world around them.

Ecosystem Composite term for a group of living organisms and their environment, and the relationship between them. Examples are a sea, a lake, a mountain and a forest.

Emergent (or marginal) plant A plant that grows at the very edge of the pond, in shallow water or in boggy soil.

Environmentally friendly Describes a way of living, a garden and/or a procedure that is in tune with the environment.

Evergreen Describes plants that retain their leaves for more than one growing season.

Exotic Strange and/or unusual; not native to an area or country.

Food animal or plant Animal or plant that provides a food source for another animal or plant.

Food chain Sequence of organisms that feed on one another in turn, with lower organisms becoming prey to higher organisms; for example, owls eat mice, mice eat slugs and worms, slugs and worms eat plants.

Green Describes people, systems, groups and ideas that are thought to be eco-friendly.

Ground cover Plants that grow swiftly to cover bare ground.

Habitat Area or environment where animals or organisms live out their lives, a place that provides all the requirements for survival.

Hedgerow Line of bushes, shrubs or trees, usually with a bank or ditch at its foot.

Hide Place of concealment used when observing wildlife; this could be a tent, shed, secluded seat or anywhere where you can sit quietly in comfort but out of view.

Host Plant or animal that in some way supports another (usually parasitic) species.

Indicator Plant or animal that in some way indicates that a wildlife area is in good health.

Introduced Describes plants or animals that have been brought in to an area by humans and are not native to that area, such as rabbits in Australia.

Invertebrate Animal without a backbone.

Leaf litter Layer of leaves, usually under trees and bushes.

Life cycle The entire development of a creature from birth to death, and the stages that it passes through.

Log garden Logs left to rot in order to provide a habitat for other creatures.

Marginal plant See Emergent (or marginal) plant.

Meadow-stream garden Garden designed and built around a slow-running, meandering stream. The meander and the slow movement of water provide a setting for specific plants and wildlife that are quite different from those living near a fast-running stream.

Migrant or migratory Describes wildlife, such as swallows, that moves from one place to another in certain seasons.

Moisture-loving plant Plant that thrives in moist soil.

Mulch Covering of bark chippings, pebbles, sheet plastic, manure or other material, applied in a layer over the soil in order to conserve moisture and cut back on weed growth.

Nocturnal Describes creatures that are active during the night, such as bats and owls.

Organic Describes a cycle where dead plants and animals become part of future organisms.

Oxygenator or oxygenating plant Plant that releases oxygen into the water. The foliage of such plants sometimes, but not always, breaks the surface of the water. In general terms, the foliage gives off bubbles of oxygen and the roots use up waste nutrients.

Perennial Plant, usually woody or herbaceous, that lives for three or more seasons.

Predator Organism that feeds on another organism.

Prey Organism that becomes food for another organism.

Submerged plant Plant that grows beneath the water in a pond or stream.

Supplementary feeding Using shop-bought bird food such as peanuts and seeds.

Sustainable Describes a process, resource or activity that can be repeated indefinitely.

Visitor Animal that appears in the garden for some part of its life, such as a moth or a fox.

Water table Natural or constant level of water in the soil below which the water will not drain away. To find the water table, dig holes in various parts of your garden, over a three-year period, in winter, spring, high summer and autumn, and keep a record of how far the surface of the water is below ground level.

Wildlife areas Areas in the garden that are given over to wildlife.

Wildlife-friendly Describes a situation, system or action that in some way positively encourages wildlife to thrive.

Wildlife water garden Natural-looking garden that is designed to attract and nurture wildlife such as birds, bugs and mammals.

Index

Acknowledgments

Photographs: iStock (pages 12, 17BR, 26, 28, 29, 35, 38, 39, 43, 46, 51, 52, 53, 56, 60, 61, 62, 63, 67CL, 72, 73, 74 and 78),
John Freeman (pages 2 and 17CL), Lorraine Harrison (page 13T) and Stephen Evans (back of cover and pages 17TL, 22 and 57TR).
Other photographs by AG&G Books.